NAMES OF
ISRAEL

NAMES OF ISRAEL

JOHN KOESSLER

MOODY PRESS
CHICAGO

© 1998 by
JOHN M. KOESSLER

All rights reserved. No part of this book may be reproduced in
any form without permission in writing from the publisher, except in the case of brief quotations embodied in critical articles
or reviews.

All Scripture quotations, unless indicated, are taken from the
Holy Bible: New International Version.® NIV.® Copyright ©
1973, 1978, 1984 by International Bible Society. Used by permission of Zondervan Publishing House. All rights reserved.

The "NIV" and "New International Version" trademarks are
registered in the United States Patent and Trademark Office by
International Bible Society. Use of either trademark requires
permission of International Bible Society.

ISBN: 0-8024-6182-4

1 3 5 7 9 10 8 6 4 2

Printed in the United States of America

To my sons Andrew and Jarred,
with love and gratitude
for all the joy they give me.

CONTENTS

INTRODUCTION

Oliver Wendell Holmes once commented that all trees live "a strange underground life": "These great fluttering masses of leaves, stems, boughs, trunks, are not the real trees. They live underground, and what we see are nothing more or less than their tails." According to Holmes, the real beauty of a tree is that "all its intelligence is in its roots. All the senses it has are in its roots." He might have been describing the church. All Christians have an important "root system" that serves to strengthen them in their walk with God. This lifeline is so important that the apostle Paul warned us never to forget its existence. It is the root system of God's Old Testament people Israel.

Paul compared God's acceptance of the Gentiles through faith in Christ to the grafting of a wild branch into an olive tree, and he observed that Christians "now share in the nourishing sap from the olive root" (Romans 11:17).

Why should Christians be interested in the many names God has used for Israel? First, we share an important privilege with the people of Israel. In all of human history there have only been two groups of people that God has chosen to identify as His very own. The first was the nation of Israel. The second was the church. God's Old Testament people are our spiritual kindred. Their history is the history of our own family of faith.

Second, we should be interested in the names of Israel because they can help us to better understand how God has dealt with us. There are many parallels between God's treatment of His people in the Old Testament and those in the New. Indeed, several of the titles that were originally applied to Israel in the Old Testament are also applied to the church.

Finally, it is important to study the names of Israel because these names provide a link to many of the promises upon which we now depend. Like the roots of a great tree that grip the earth and hold it in place, these promises provide security and can become a channel of spiritual life. The Old Testament will always be relevant for Christians. It was the church's first Bible. The things written in it were preserved for our benefit both as an encouragement and a warning (1 Corinthians 10:11). It is my prayer that as you learn about the names of Israel, you will also hear God's still, quiet voice calling you by name.

1
ISRAEL

Then the man said, "Your name will no longer be Jacob, but Israel, because you have struggled with God and with men and have overcome." *(Genesis 32:28)*

"Take that back or I'll punch you in the nose!"
"You will not!"
"I will too!"

It wasn't that I thought my brother couldn't do it. The two of us had sparred before. I just didn't think that he would hit me in my uncle's living room. I was wrong. My dare was all he needed to spur him on. As soon as the words were out of my mouth, I found myself toppling backward, propelled over the rocking chair by his sturdy left jab. As I sat dazed on the floor, he declared triumphantly, "I told you I would do it!"

My brother and I were not unusual. Even in the best families, brothers don't always agree. The Bible is full of similar examples. However, the conflict between Jacob and Esau, the grandsons of the patriarch Abraham, was remarkable. For one thing, it was longer than most. It started even before the two brothers were born, as Isaac's twin sons wrestled with each other in the womb (Genesis 25:22). The struggle between them was symbolized in birth, when Jacob emerged from the womb grasping the heel of his older brother (v. 26). Because of this, his parents gave him a name that portrayed Jacob as a wrestler who had tripped his opponent by the heels.

The Hebrew root upon which Jacob's name was based also meant "to deceive" and foreshadowed the ruse Jacob would use to trick his father into giving him the blessing that Isaac had originally intended for Esau. Taking advantage of his aged father's blindness, Jacob disguised himself as Esau and lied to Isaac. When Esau discovered what his brother had done, he said: "Isn't he rightly named Jacob? He has deceived me these two times: He took my birthright, and now he's taken my blessing!" (Genesis 27:36).

Long-standing feuds between siblings usually don't end easily, and the dispute between Isaac's sons was no exception. Knowing that Esau would eventually attempt to kill Jacob, Rebekah sent him to stay with her brother Laban in Haran. This exile served two purposes. The separation between the brothers gave Esau time to cool off and provided Jacob with an opportunity to look for a wife among those who shared his religious heritage.

It was a different Jacob who made his way back home twenty years later. During his stay in Haran he had married and had children. He had become a financial success, acquiring flocks and herds, but he continued to wrestle in his relationships. His partnership with his father-in-law was a stormy one that ended when Jacob packed up all he had and literally headed for the hills (Genesis 31:21). The one who had been labeled a deceiver by his twin brother had learned what it was like to have the tables turned. Laban had repeatedly broken his promises to Jacob and changed his wages (Genesis 31:38–42). The final parting between them was tense. Laban had pursued Jacob with a small army and finally left him with a benediction that was more of a threat than a blessing (Genesis 31:48–50).

Jacob's marital life was also a struggle. Laban had tricked Jacob into marrying a woman he did not love and then forced him to work an additional seven years for the one he really wanted to marry. Jacob's two wives competed with each other to see who could have more children, thinking that this would earn their husband's affection (Genesis 29:31–30:24).

Despite these problems, it was Esau who plagued Jacob's thoughts as he slept on the bank of the Jabbok River. Twenty years had passed since they had last seen each other. Word had reached Jacob that Esau was coming to meet him with four hundred men. Such a large number could mean only one thing: Esau intended to make good on his threat to kill his brother! Jacob did what he could to mollify the situation. He divided his family into two camps, hoping that if one were to be attacked the other would have a chance to escape. He also sent portions of his flocks and herds on ahead as a present, putting space between them so that Esau would receive them in stages. This was really a kind of restitution. It allowed Jacob to return to Esau some of the blessings that he had lost.

The most important thing that Jacob did that night was pray. In his prayer he reminded God of two things. The first was that Jacob had been commanded to return to his country and his family. The threat that he faced had come about as a consequence of his obedience. Second, he reminded God of His promise to bless Jacob and make his descendants as numerous as the sand of the sea (Genesis

32:9–12). This was the same promise that had been
made to Jacob's grandfather Abraham and his father
Isaac (Genesis 22:17; 26:4). Jacob also expressed
appreciation for God's grace. He admitted that he
did not deserve any of the blessings that had come
to him, and he prayed for God's protection (Genesis
32:9–11).

God sent a single angel in answer to Jacob's
prayer. But instead of attacking Esau's men, the angel wrestled with Jacob. Moreover, this was no
ordinary angel. According to the prophet Hosea,
when Jacob wrestled with the angel, he was really
struggling with God (Hosea 12:3–4). Many biblical
scholars believe that this being, known as the Angel
of the Lord, was really a manifestation of Christ in
human form prior to the Incarnation.

The match was finally decided when the Angel
of the Lord touched the socket of Jacob's hip and
wrenched it out of joint. Although defeated, Jacob
continued to wrestle, pleading with the Angel of
the Lord for a blessing. God answered Jacob's
prayer, but probably not in the way the patriarch
had expected. He changed the patriarch's name
from Jacob to Israel. Derived from a Hebrew verb
that meant "to strive," this name could be literally
translated "he contends with God," or possibly, "let
God contend." It was the name that would be given
to Jacob's descendants. When Esau's men finally
came into view, the man who limped out to meet
them was radically changed. The two brothers em-
braced and a lifetime of bitterness was finally
reconciled.

Jacob's experience is a reminder that we win
only when we allow God to have the victory in our

lives. Throughout his many struggles, Jacob had proved to be his own worst enemy. God used His word, His power, and an entire lifetime of circumstances to transform the man who had been nicknamed "the deceiver." God uses the same tools to change us into the image of Christ. Could it be that many of the struggles you now face are really a reflection of your own wrestling match with God?

God of Jacob, touch my life in such a way that every step I take reflects Your power. Humble me by Your gentle hand. Amen.

2
MY PEOPLE

The Lord said, "I have indeed seen the misery of my people in Egypt. I have heard them crying out because of their slave drivers, and I am concerned about their suffering." (*Exodus 3:7*)

If you were granted a personal audience with God and could only ask one question, what would it be? It would have been an easy choice for Moses. As a young man he had dreamed of being the one who would rescue Israel from slavery in Egypt (Acts 7:25). When his first attempt ended in disaster, Moses fled into the wilderness and spent the next forty years in exile. During that time he married, had children, and worked as a shepherd watching over the flocks of his father-in-law. There he pondered the same question that his countrymen had voiced so often to God during their entire time in bondage: Why didn't God seem to care about the sufferings of His people?

The answer came in an unexpected form. While tending the flocks in a remote part of the desert near Mount Horeb, Moses noticed a burning bush. Although it was engulfed in flames, the bush did not appear to be harmed. Intrigued, Moses came closer to inspect this unusual sight and heard the voice of God speaking to him from within the bush. In His message God assured Moses of three things. First, the Lord told Moses that He had seen Israel's misery. The Hebrew grammar places an emphasis on this statement. The message to Moses and Israel was not merely, "I have seen" but rather, "I have most certainly seen the suffering of My people." It was important that God's suffering people know that their pain was not hidden from view.

Second, God assured Moses that He had "heard" Israel's cry. He knew of their circumstances and was listening to their prayers. These were no ordinary cries. The Hebrew term that is translated "crying out" refers to a loud cry of distress. This was not a carefully crafted and articulate prayer so much as it was a cry of pain so deep that it sounded like the bellowing of a wounded animal. Elsewhere the same word is used to describe the cry of a woman who is being raped (Deuteronomy 22:24).

Third, the Lord told Moses that He was concerned about Israel's suffering. This was really a summary explanation based upon the previous two assurances. God had seen Israel's misery and had listened to their desperate cries precisely because He cared about their suffering. God had watched with deep concern as their taskmasters had worked them to death. When the Egyptian whips cut into their flesh and they cried out in pain, God heard the sound. Even when they were completely unaware of Him, they continued to receive His undivided attention. This was because God had bound Himself to Israel when He made a covenant with their ancestor Abraham.

The things that they were suffering had not come as a surprise to God. He had even warned Abraham in advance of the things that Israel would suffer: "Then the Lord said to him, 'Know for certain that your descendants will be strangers in a country not their own, and they will be enslaved and mistreated four hundred years. But I will punish the nation they serve as slaves, and afterward they will come out with great possessions' " (Genesis 15:13–14). God's eyes were open, His ears were tuned to their cry, and the clock was set for the time of their deliverance.

God's interest in His people reflected a very special kind of concern. The Hebrew text uses the verb "to know" to describe it. This term spoke of an awareness that was so deep that it could normally be gained only by experience. This same concern would later motivate Jesus Christ to experience temptation, in order to be able to sympathize with the sufferings of His people: "For we do not have a high priest who is unable to sympathize with our weaknesses, but we have one who has been tempted in every way, just as we are—yet was without sin" (Hebrews 4:15). In this respect the church stands on even firmer ground than Israel did. Like the Israelites, we have God's promise that He understands our suffering. However, we also have Christ's living example. Because He has shared our experience, He knows how to help us in our moment of need. Christ's words to the churches in the book of Revelation assure suffering, tempted, and even disobedient believers that He is able to understand their plight. He repeatedly says: "I know . . . I know . . . I know" (Revelation 2:2, 9, 13, 19; 3:1, 8).

In his autobiography, Holocaust survivor Elie Wiesel recounts the story of a group of Jews who were forced to hide in an underground shelter beneath a synagogue in Mainz during the Crusades. One night two rabbis heard sounds coming from the synagogue above them and went to investigate. They saw no one but heard voices speaking out of the darkness. Sensing God's presence, the two rabbis fell to their knees and began to pray: "Is it You, Lord, who wish our death? Have You changed sides? Have You decided to anoint the enemy as Your chosen people?"[1]

One can hear a similar cry behind each of the assurances made to Moses. It is the echo of the frustrated prayer uttered by any believer who has ever suffered: "God, can't You see what is happening to me? Aren't You listening to my prayers? Don't You care?"

God's reply is a resounding "Yes!" He cannot help caring. We are His people.

Compassionate Father, I thank You that You understand my need and hear my prayers. Help me to trust in You in spite of my circumstances. Amen.

1. Elie Wiesel, *Memoirs: All Rivers Run to the Sea* (New York: Knopf, 1995), 83–84.

3
THE HEBREWS

The elders of Israel will listen to you.
Then you and the elders are to go to the king
of Egypt and say to him, "The Lord, the God
of the Hebrews, has met with us. Let us take
a three-day journey into the desert to offer
sacrifices to the Lord our God." (Exodus 3:18)

A cartoon by artist Bill Mauldin showed Willie
and Joe, the two dogfaced GIs whose exploits
he made famous in armed forces newspapers during World War II, standing on the corner of a
village in France. As they watch the French women
and the men in berets pass by, Willie turns to his
partner and says: "Did ya ever see so many fur-
riners, Joe?" Their thinking is typical. We don't
usually consider ourselves to be "foreigners," even
when we are in another country. Yet that is exactly
what the name "Hebrew" emphasized when it was
applied to the descendants of Abraham.

The etymology of the term "Hebrew" is uncertain. Many Bible scholars believe that it came from
a Hebrew root that meant "cross over" or "go beyond." If this is true, the reference in Genesis 14:13
to "Abram the Hebrew" could roughly mean "Abram
from across the river." Others have suggested that
the term was originally derisive and meant "bound-
ary jumper." They believe it was used to identify
the Israelites as trespassers. Another theory suggests that the term came from the name Eber, one
of Shem's descendants. This would identify the He-

brews as the descendants of Eber (Genesis 10:21).

What is clear is that the term "Hebrew" was used as an ethnic label to distinguish the Israelites from those around them. It was used by Israelites and non-Israelites alike.

When Joseph explained his plight to the chief cupbearer while in prison, he complained that he had been "forcibly carried off from the land of the Hebrews" (Genesis 40:15). When the infant Moses was discovered floating among the reeds in a basket, Pharaoh's daughter recognized that he was "one of the Hebrew babies" that her father had commanded to be drowned in the Nile (Exodus 2:6). The Philistines also referred to the Israelites as Hebrews (1 Samuel 4:6, 9).

In the New Testament, the apostle Paul referred to himself as a "Hebrew" and as a "Hebrew of Hebrews" (2 Corinthians 11:22; Philippians 3:5). In both instances he used the term to describe his own religious and ethnic heritage. In particular, it identified Paul as a Jew who clung to the language and traditions of Hebrew culture rather than adopting the customs of the Greeks. Similarly, there were synagogues in Rome and Corinth that were labeled by those who attended them as synagogues "of the Hebrews."

This title was a source of pride to those who could claim it. In fact, one of the earliest disputes in the church involved a conflict between the Grecian Jews and the Hebraic Jews because the Greek-speaking widows were being neglected in the daily distribution of food (Acts 6:1). This may have reflected an attitude of superiority among those who identified themselves as Hebrews. The apostle Paul listed this heritage as one of the factors in his past that might have given him reason to put confidence in the flesh (Philippians 3:4–5).

Paul had been a Pharisee, one of the strictest sects of Palestinian Judaism. He had also studied under Gamaliel, one of the leading teachers of his day and the grandson of the great rabbi Hillel. Although Paul valued this heritage, he did not consider it to be an advantage when compared to the knowledge of Christ:

> But whatever was to my profit I now consider loss for the sake of Christ. What is more, I consider everything a loss compared to the surpassing greatness of knowing Christ Jesus my Lord, for whose sake I have lost all things. I consider them rubbish, that I may gain Christ and be found in him, not having a righteousness of my own that comes from the law, but that which is through faith in Christ—the righteousness that comes from God and is by faith. (Philippians 3:7–9)

Through faith in Christ it is possible for us to say that the God of the Hebrews, the same God who rescued Israel from slavery in Egypt, is also our God. However, Paul's refusal to boast in the fact that he was a "Hebrew of the Hebrews" is a warning that even a Christian religious heritage is of little value if it is not grounded in genuine faith. Today many people take pride in the fact that they were baptized into a certain religious tradition or have attended Sunday school since their childhood, but they have never trusted in Jesus Christ for eternal life. They have known about Christ all their lives, but they do not know Christ personally.

The Scriptures affirm the value of a godly heritage. One of the strengths that the apostle Paul saw
in his colleague Timothy was the fact that he had
been taught the Scriptures from infancy (2 Timothy
3:15). Yet Timothy did not rely on his religious heritage; he knew Christ personally. Only those who
have received Christ by faith have the right to claim
the title "child of God." This status can only be
claimed individually by faith by each succeeding
generation and cannot be passed down through the
family line (John 1:12–13).

In addition, the use of the term "Hebrews" to
distinguish the Israelites from the Gentile world
around them is a reminder that God's people will always stand out from the rest of society. Those of us
who know Christ as Savior are "foreigners" where
this world is concerned. Our commitment to Christ
will cause us to stand out in our community, on our
block, and perhaps even in our own family. We
should not be afraid to live as "aliens and strangers."
This same difference will attract interest in the
gospel and will ultimately bring glory to God: "Dear
friends, I urge you, as aliens and strangers in the
world, to abstain from sinful desires, which war
against your soul. Live such good lives among the
pagans that, though they accuse you of doing
wrong, they may see your good deeds and glorify
God on the day he visits us" (1 Peter 2:11–12).

*God of the Hebrews, I am grateful that You are my
God through faith in Jesus Christ. Thank You for rescuing me from slavery to sin so that I might be able to
serve You. Help me to live as a "foreigner" as far as the
ungodly practices of this world are concerned. Amen.*

4

MY FIRSTBORN SON

> Then say to Pharaoh, "This is what the
> Lord says: Israel is my firstborn son, and I
> told you, 'Let my son go, so he may worship
> me.' But you refused to let him go; so I will
> kill your firstborn son." (Exodus 4:22–23)

The moment the nurse handed me my firstborn
son, I knew my life had changed forever. As I
held him close to my chest, a squirming bundle of
life tightly wrapped in a blanket, I wondered if he
could hear the nervous beating of my heart. I had
seen hundreds of babies in my life. Some seemed
cute and others homely. I had heard them laugh
and cry. But I had never seen a baby like this. This
one was mine!

My excitement was tempered with a measure
of fear when we finally carried him across the
threshold of our home and laid him in his bed for
the first time. We were suddenly aware that his welfare now depended entirely on us. There were no
buttons to push and no nurses to call when we
couldn't figure out why his crying wouldn't stop.
We dragged his crib into our bedroom to be as
close to him as we could during the night, but we
found that we couldn't sleep as long as he was
there. The slightest rustle woke us. We both
strained our ears to hear and diagnose the smallest
sigh that emanated from him.

For the people of Israel, the birth of one's firstborn child brought a similar excitement but a

different kind of fear. For them, the firstborn child was a solemn reminder of the cost of their redemption. In the Law of Moses God's people were told: "Consecrate to me every firstborn male. The first offspring of every womb among the Israelites belongs to me, whether man or animal" (Exodus 13:2). This command was given soon after the Israelites left Egypt. It commemorated the fact that God had delivered them by slaying all the firstborn of the Egyptians. As a result all the firstborn, whether animal or human, were regarded as God's property. The firstborn of animals considered to be ceremonially clean were sacrificed. Unclean animals were "redeemed" by offering a lamb as a substitute. Since human sacrifices were an abomination to God, the firstborn were similarly redeemed, and later the Levites were consecrated to God in place of Israel's firstborn (Numbers 3:11–13).

The consecration of Israel's firstborn symbolized the fact that God considered all Israel as belonging to Him. When Moses confronted Pharaoh just prior to the final plague, the message he had been ordered to deliver contained a sobering threat: "Then say to Pharaoh, 'This is what the Lord says: Israel is my firstborn son, and I told you, "Let my son go, so he may worship me." But you refused to let him go; so I will kill your firstborn son' " (Exodus 4:22–23).

Every firstborn son was a reminder of three important truths. First, he was a reminder that Israel owed its existence to the death of another. The offering of a lamb as a substitute for each child implied that the life of the firstborn was forfeit. The death of Egypt's firstborn was the stroke that finally persuaded Pharaoh to set Israel free as God had commanded. In a sense, the blood of others had been shed to earn God's people their freedom. It was also blood that had protected them on that terrible night when the Angel of Death entered the Egyptians' homes and took the life of every firstborn. During the night a pitiful cry was heard as wails of mourning rang out from each household, joining together in a haunting chorus of grief (Exodus 12:30). Meanwhile, Israelites huddled together around the Passover lamb, protected by the blood that covered the door post and lintel.

This event foreshadowed the coming of Jesus Christ, who is the true Passover sacrifice (1 Corinthians 5:7). Like the blood of the sacrificial lamb, Christ's blood marks those who have trusted in Him as the objects of God's mercy. They are kept from judgment because Jesus is "the Lamb of God, who takes away the sin of the world" (John 1:29).

Second, the birth of a firstborn child was a reminder of God's grace. The terrifying judgments that had fallen on the Egyptians not only proved the superiority of Israel's God over the false gods of Egypt, but they also set the Israelites apart as a nation. After the third plague, each time the hand of God dealt its blow the Egyptians saw the Israelites spared. Later, the Israelites were told that God's choice of Israel was based upon His love (Deuteronomy 7:7–9). Like Israel, those of us who have trusted in Christ are also protected from judgment by God's grace. We are "shielded by God's power" through faith in Christ's saving work (1 Peter 1:5).

Third, the birth of a firstborn child was a reminder that God's people had been called to be living sacrifices. Those who were consecrated to God were really representative of the entire community. It was not merely the firstborn that belonged to God, but the nation as a whole. When God commanded Pharaoh to free the Israelites, He referred to the entire nation as "my firstborn son." All Israelites were called to be holy before God (Exodus 19:5–6; 22:31). The consecration of the firstborn was a vivid testimony to God's ownership of all Israel.

The title "firstborn" was used by New Testament writers to emphasize Christ's uniqueness. According to Romans 8:29, God has predestined believers to be conformed to the likeness of Christ so that "he might be the firstborn among many brothers." Jesus Christ is supreme over all creation because He is "the firstborn" (Colossians 1:15). This does not mean that Jesus was a created being but that He is superior to all things as Creator. It is a title that emphasizes Christ's preeminence and His special relationship to the Father. Jesus is also called the firstborn because of the resurrection (Colossians 1:18; Revelation 1:5).

The title of "firstborn" was also used by the writer of the book of Hebrews to refer to believers. Those who belong to Christ are called "the church of the firstborn, whose names are written in heaven" (Hebrews 12:23). As He did for the Israelites when He rescued them from Egypt, God purchased the church for Himself through the saving work of Christ. As precious as my first child was and is to me, Christ's death and resurrection prove that I am even more precious to God.

Heavenly Father, I thank You for the work of Jesus Christ and for the fact that my name is written in heaven. I consecrate myself to You today as a living sacrifice and offer all that I think, say, and do for Your glory. Amen.

5

THE COMMUNITY OF ISRAEL

For seven days no yeast is to be found in your houses. And whoever eats anything with yeast in it must be cut off from the community of Israel, whether he is an alien or native-born. (*Exodus 12:19*)

E very year when the weather becomes warmer, countless households go through the ritual of spring cleaning. Basements and garages are cleared out, curtains are taken to the cleaners, and walls are washed. The Feast of Unleavened Bread enabled the Israelites to do a different kind of housecleaning. As part of their preparation for the observance of Passover, Israelites were required to remove all leaven from their homes (Exodus 13:7). This action symbolized their need to do spiritual housecleaning.

Leaven was usually a piece of leftover dough that had fermented and functioned like yeast. It was added to bread to make it rise. The use of unleavened bread at the original Passover signified Israel's haste in leaving Egypt (Exodus 12:39). Jesus used leaven to illustrate the nature of the kingdom of God (Luke 13:21). He also used it as a symbol of corruption and warned His disciples to be on guard against the "yeast of the Pharisees and Sadducees" (Matthew 16:6).

It is significant that the Feast of Unleavened Bread was a congregational celebration. Every household was required to observe it, and those who refused were to be excluded from the congregation. The Hebrew term that is translated "community" in Exodus 12:19 comes from a verb that meant "to appoint." It described the congregation or community of Israel as those who had been called together by God for a purpose.

The concept of community is foundational to biblical spirituality. Throughout the Old Testament the spiritual life of the individual was linked to that of the community. One of the most vivid examples of this was seen in Israel's defeat at the battle of Ai. When Achan sinned by taking items that God had said should be destroyed, the entire community suffered. Even though only one man disobeyed God's command, Joshua 7:1 described the sin in terms that implied that the whole congregation was accountable: "But the Israelites acted unfaithfully in regard to the devoted things. Achan son of Carmi . . . of the tribe of Judah, took some of them. So the Lord's anger burned against Israel."

This corporate dimension to the believer's spiritual life was also reflected in the New Testament. The apostle Paul compared the church to a body and noted that the church as a whole is affected by the state of any one member (1 Corinthians 12:26). When the Corinthian church was unwilling to discipline one of its members who had become involved in sexual immorality, he warned of sin's potential to act like leaven:

> Your boasting is not good. Don't you know that a little yeast works through the whole batch of dough? Get rid of the old yeast that you may be a new batch without yeast—as you really are. For Christ, our Passover lamb, has been sacrificed. Therefore let us keep the Fes-

> *tival, not with the old yeast, the yeast of malice and wickedness, but with bread without yeast, the bread of sincerity and truth. (1 Corinthians 5:6–8)*

Paul's analogy was based on the practice of purging leaven from Israelite homes prior to the Feast of Unleavened Bread. His illustration was especially appropriate in view of the command to expel those who refused to do so from the community. He had similarly urged the Corinthians to "expel the wicked man from among you" (1 Corinthians 5:13). The man's refusal to repent indicated that he had refused to purge the leaven of sin from his life. As a result he was to be excluded from the community of believers.

It is important to remember, however, that it was sin and not the erring believer that Paul saw as leaven. His call for expulsion from the congregation was intended to be redemptive. After his removal from the Corinthian church, the believer Paul had excommunicated repented. Paul wrote to the church again and urged that this same man be accepted back into the fellowship: "The punishment inflicted on him by the majority is sufficient for him. Now instead, you ought to forgive and comfort him, so that he will not be overwhelmed by excessive sorrow" (2 Corinthians 2:6–7).

The church of today seems to vacillate between two unhealthy extremes when it comes to the practice of church discipline. Often congregations ignore the sin of their members, considering it a purely private matter. They view those who exercise church discipline to be "too legalistic" and judgmental. This view fails to recognize that the church has a responsibility to exercise a kind of judgment where its members are concerned (1 Corinthians 5:12). The other extreme is to excommunicate members for minor offenses or to exercise church discipline without making restoration the goal.

Although every sin is serious, not all are worthy of excommunication. The conflict between Euodia and Syntyche in the church at Philippi was so great that Paul urged believers in that church to help them reconcile with each other. He did not, however, call for their expulsion from the congregation. The apostle John described a case where a church leader was excommunicating others for selfish motives:

> *I wrote to the church, but Diotrephes, who loves to be first, will have nothing to do with us. So if I come, I will call attention to what he is doing, gossiping maliciously about us. Not satisfied with that, he refuses to welcome the brothers. He also stops those who want to do so and puts them out of the church. (3 John 9–10)*

In John's case it was the leader doing the excommunicating who really needed to be disciplined!

We all need to engage in a little spiritual housecleaning now and then. This is the best way to ensure that church discipline will not be needed. Got any leaven lying around the house?

Holy Spirit, search my life. Shine the light of Your Word into my heart and help me to clear out any "leaven" that might be there. Amen.

6

A STIFF-NECKED PEOPLE

"I have seen these people," the Lord said to
Moses, "and they are a stiff-necked people."
(Exodus 32:9)

Stubbornness can sometimes be an asset. Children's author Dr. Seuss was rejected twenty-three
times before being given a contract for his first
book—which went on to sell more than 6 million
copies. Inventor Thomas Edison performed fifty
thousand failed experiments before achieving success in finding a new storage battery. After Louis B.
Mayer turned down Greta Garbo's request for a
raise, the actress went back to her hotel and stayed
there until Mayer finally gave in—it took seven
months. Michael Jordan was cut from his high
school basketball team but went on to become one
of the greatest players in the history of the NBA.

When it comes to our relationship with God,
however, stubbornness is often a hindrance. One of
the Lord's primary complaints against the nation of
Israel was that they were a "stiff-necked people."
This description compared the attitude of Israel to
an animal that stiffened its neck to resist the tug of
the reins or the placement of the yoke. It was a picture of unbending resistance to the will of God.

The first time God used this label to describe
His people was while Moses was receiving the Law
on Mount Sinai. Unsure of what to make of his ab-
sence for forty days, the people ordered Aaron to
make an idol (Exodus 32:1). Days earlier they had

heard the voice of God speaking to Moses. Among the commandments was this foundational prohibition against idolatry: "You shall not make for yourself an idol in the form of anything in heaven above or on the earth beneath or in the waters below" (Exodus 20:4).

This sin came to be seen as the most notorious action in their history. It was the low point by which all other spiritual declines were measured. The people's demand for an idol was based upon a desire to worship a god who would "go before" them. Ironically, this was precisely what the Lord had done ever since they departed from Egypt: "By day the Lord went ahead of them in a pillar of cloud to guide them on their way and by night in a pillar of fire to give them light, so that they could travel by day or night. Neither the pillar of cloud by day nor the pillar of fire by night left its place in front of the people" (Exodus 13:21–22).

Their basic desire was a legitimate one. They wanted a god that they could worship and one who would lead them to the land of promise. Unfortunately they wanted these things on their own terms rather than on God's terms. They wanted a god who was tangible and visible. They wanted to experience the blessings that had been promised to them, but they didn't want to wait for God's timetable.

In a very real sense, this sin was the prototype of all Israel's later sins. It also reflects the pattern for our own sins. Sin is really just an attempt to get the things that only God can provide from some other source and on our own terms. We commit immorality because we want to feel accepted and loved. We get drunk because we want to experience peace and joy. We lie and exaggerate because we want to feel worthwhile. The sad reality, of course, is that sin never comes through on its false promises. It may give the illusion that it can fulfill our needs, just as the Israelites may have been able to fool themselves as they looked at the golden statue they carried at the head of their procession. But in the end their false god couldn't lead them where they wanted to go.

Being "stiff-necked" is as much an individual sin as a corporate one. It was the sin committed by Zedekiah, the last king of Judah, when he refused to listen and to humble himself and return to the Lord after hearing the words of the prophet Jeremiah (2 Chronicles 36:13; cf. Jeremiah 37:2). Zedekiah asked Jeremiah for prayers and sought his counsel (Jeremiah 37:2–3, 17). However, even though God promised him safety if he surrendered to the officers of the king of Babylon, he refused to obey because of his fear that others would hand him over to his enemies for mistreatment (Jeremiah 38:17–19). Despite repeated warnings from God that he should surrender peacefully to the Babylonians, he tried to escape when Jerusalem was finally taken. He was captured, blinded, and carried to Babylon in bronze shackles (Jeremiah 39:5–7). Zedekiah is a good example of the kind of person the writer of Proverbs described when he warned: "A man who remains stiff-necked after many rebukes will suddenly be destroyed—without remedy" (Proverbs 29:1). Although interested in God's word and willing to listen to it, he was too stubborn to change his plans.

The right kind of stubbornness might be better described as determination. The biblical terms for this characteristic are "perseverance" and "endurance." In several areas of life this godly stubbornness is especially important. One of the most critical is the area of prayer. Believers are to "be alert and always keep on praying for all the saints" (Ephesians 6:18). Prayer is difficult at times and its answers are not always as speedy as we would like. Effective prayer requires a willingness to persevere until God responds. Jesus taught His disciples to emulate the persistent widow who refused to be put off by the judge's unwillingness to respond to her pleas (Luke 18:1–8). He did not mean to imply that God is unwilling to hear our prayers, but that God's eagerness to respond makes an answer all the more certain. Godly stubbornness is also needed when facing difficult circumstances. The apostle Paul linked these two areas together in Romans 12:12 when he commanded his readers to be "joyful in hope, patient in affliction, faithful in prayer."

This kind of determination takes more than human will power. Ultimately, the ability to persevere is a work of God's grace (Colossians 1:11). It is produced through the experience of tribulation but is not an end in itself. Perseverance leads to godly character, which is the visible evidence that God is at work transforming the believer's life (Romans 5:3–5).

Determination can be a key to either success or failure. If it is prompted by the Holy Spirit and subject to God's Word, it will lead to success. But when it is rooted in pride and guided by self-will, we follow in the footsteps of those Israelites who wanted to worship gods of their own making more than the Creator who redeemed them.

Holy Spirit, work through the trials that I am facing today to produce the fruit of perseverance and godly character. Root out any stubbornness that threatens to turn my heart from the living God. Amen.

7

MY SERVANTS

> Even if he is not redeemed in any of these
> ways, he and his children are to be released
> in the Year of Jubilee, for the Israelites belong
> to me as servants. They are my servants,
> whom I brought out of Egypt. I am the Lord
> your God. (*Leviticus 25:54–55*)

Abraham Lincoln once said that he was opposed
to slavery because it did not allow those who
suffered under it to better their condition. "I like
the system which lets a man quit when he wants to,
and wish it might prevail everywhere," he explained. "What is the true condition of the laborer?
I take it that it is best for all to leave each man free
to acquire property as fast as he can. Some will get
wealthy. I don't believe in a law to prevent a man
from getting rich; it would do more harm than
good."

Lincoln's opposition to slavery was based upon
economic and political convictions. His primary
concern when he freed the slaves was not the aboli-
tion of slavery, so much as it was the preservation of
the Union. Some may be surprised and even disturbed at the pragmatic tone expressed by the
author of the Emancipation Proclamation in a letter
to Horace Greeley written in 1862: "My paramount
object in this struggle is to save the Union, and is
not either to save or destroy Slavery. If I could save
the Union without freeing any slave, I would do it;
and if I could save it by freeing all the slaves, I

would do it; and if I could do it by freeing some
and leaving others alone, I would also do that."

Some find the Old Testament's pragmatic approach to slavery equally disturbing. They are
troubled by the fact that the Bible does not explic-
itly condemn the practice of slavery. It is important
to recognize, however, that God's law did not institute slavery. It merely regulated an already existing
practice. The Scriptures never commanded God's
people to become slaves, nor did they ever tell
them to take slaves, except in the case of a thief
who was unable to pay for what he had stolen. In
this instance the sentence of slavery allowed the
thief to make restitution for what had been taken
(Exodus 22:3). In other cases the biblical laws regarding slavery were actually protective. For
example, Hebrew slaves were only permitted to
serve for six years and then were to go free (Exodus
21:2; Deuteronomy 15:12). In the Year of Jubilee,
held every fiftieth year, all Hebrew slaves were freed,
regardless of the number of years left of their servi-
tude (Leviticus 25:39–41). In this respect, Hebrew
slaves were really more like indentured servants.
They were not to be treated as slaves by the Israelites
but as hired workers (Leviticus 25:40).

Another example of protective legislation can be
found in Exodus 21:7–8: "If a man sells his daughter
as a servant, she is not to go free as menservants do.
If she does not please the master who has selected
her for himself, he must let her be redeemed. He has
no right to sell her to foreigners, because he has
broken faith with her." In this case the Law's restriction was aimed at the master rather than at the
slave. This slave's role was comparable to that of a

wife, whether for the master or for one of his sons (cf. Exodus 21:9–10). The Law of Moses ordered the master to give her all the rights due to a wife or else allow her to be redeemed. Her master could not simply abandon her or sell her to foreigners.

The New Testament is also strangely silent about the practice of slavery. Instead of condemning those who owned slaves, it commanded slaves to submit to their masters (Ephesians 6:5; Colossians 3:22; 1 Timothy 6:1; Titus 2:9). Those who were able to obtain their freedom were urged to do so, but the rest were to submit with respect even when they were treated unfairly (1 Corinthians 7:21; 1 Peter 2:18). New Testament believers were warned not to become slaves, but those who were called to Christ as slaves were not to be anxious about their status (1 Corinthians 7:21–23).

Clearly these laws were not intended to create an ideal society. On occasion God appears to have tolerated and even regulated practices that He did not actually condone. Jesus alluded to this fact when He was questioned about the Old Testament law concerning divorce. According to Jesus, Moses regulated the preexisting practice of divorce without ever approving of it (Matthew 19:8–9).

God's primary reason for regulating slavery was theological rather than sociological. Israel's form of slavery provided a kind of economic safety net for those who were desperately poor among God's people. More than that, however, it provided Israel with a concrete metaphor of God's relationship with His people. The primary reason that Israelite slaves were to be freed during the Year of Jubilee was that they already belonged to another Master:

"The Israelites belong to me as servants. They are my servants, whom I brought out of Egypt. I am the Lord your God" (Leviticus 25:55).

The Bible uses similar language to describe New Testament believers. Christians have been purchased by God (Acts 20:28). According to the apostle Paul this divine ownership has very practical implications. It should be reflected in our actions: "Do you not know that your body is a temple of the Holy Spirit, who is in you, whom you have received from God? You are not your own; you were bought at a price. Therefore honor God with your body" (1 Corinthians 6:19–20). Our words and actions identify us as those who belong to Jesus Christ. Those who are not Christians look to our deeds and our speech to verify the truth of the gospel we preach. Too many of us have heard unbelievers preface their rejection of Christ with the words: "I used to know someone who believed like you do, and they . . ."

Although our actions can bring glory to God or dishonor His name, they cannot earn His favor. Jesus made this clear when He compared His followers to the servant whose actions do not merit any thanks. He explained that a servant who had been asked by the master to wait on him during dinner would not expect to receive praise for merely doing what was expected: "Would he thank the servant because he did what he was told to do? So you also, when you have done everything you were told to do, should say, 'We are unworthy servants; we have only done our duty' " (Luke 17:9–10).

No matter how much we may serve God, it is we who are the debtors. Like Israel, we have been purchased by God. He paid the highest price imaginable when He sent His Son to die for our sins. All that we do, are, and have belongs to Him.

Master and Savior, I offer myself to You today, thankful for Your grace and forgiveness. Help me so that my words and deeds will bring glory to Your name and will draw others to Jesus Christ. Amen.

8

THE COUNTLESS
THOUSANDS OF ISRAEL

Whenever the ark set out, Moses said, "Rise up, O Lord! May your enemies be scattered; may your foes flee before you." Whenever it came to rest, he said, "Return, O Lord, to the countless thousands of Israel." *(Numbers 10:35)*

George has an important job at the small Baptist church he attends each Sunday. He is the one responsible for counting everyone who is at worship and posting the attendance figures. The numbers rarely climb beyond the teens.

"When I put the numbers up," he explained, "I always add one."

"Do you do that to encourage the pastor?" I asked.

"Oh no," he answered. He seemed surprised that I would suggest such a thing.

"I always add one because I figure God is here too!"

Moses might echo George's sentiment. His joyful description of God's people as the "countless thousands of Israel" in this verse came within the context of an invitation offered to God. After an eleven-month encampment in the wilderness of Sinai, Moses and the Israelites finally set out for the wilderness of Paran. When the cloud of God's presence lifted above the tabernacle, it signaled the start of the journey. When the cloud settled, it indicated that it was time to make camp again (Numbers 9:15–23; 10:12). During their journey the Israelites carried the ark, the symbol of God's covenant, before them, while the tribes followed behind in their appointed order. Judah was in the lead, and each tribe marched beneath its own banner. When the ark set out, Moses gave this shout of victory: "Rise up, O Lord! May your enemies be scattered; may your foes flee before you." When the time came to make camp again, Moses invited God to return to fellowship with His people with the words: "Return, O Lord, to the countless thousands of Israel."

In the Hebrew text the phrase "countless thousands" is actually "ten thousand thousands." This was not a literal figure but was intended to convey an unusually large host. This description was also an acknowledgment that God had fulfilled His promises to Abraham to multiply his descendants. When the Lord told Abraham that he would be given an heir, He commanded him to look into the heavens and count the stars. As Abraham considered the impossibility of such a task, the Lord promised: "So shall your offspring be" (Genesis 15:5). Earlier, the Lord had promised to make Abraham's descendants as numerous as "the dust of the earth" (Genesis 13:16). On another occasion the Lord promised that Abraham's descendants would be as numerous as the sand on the seashore (Genesis 22:17).

These promises were repeated to Abraham's son Isaac and his grandson Jacob (Genesis 26:24; 28:14; 32:12). Jacob later entered Egypt with seventy-five people (Acts 7:14). In the years that followed, the size of the Israelite population increased so much that Pharaoh saw them as a threat and began to oppress them (Exodus 1:8–10). It was this oppression that eventually led to the Exodus. God's promises to increase Abraham's descendants were also restated through the prophet Hosea, when their fulfillment seemed threatened by the exile of Israel:

> *Yet the Israelites will be like the sand on the seashore, which cannot be measured or counted. In the place where it was said to them, 'You are not my people,' they will be called 'sons of the living God.' The people of Judah and the people of Israel will be reunited, and they will appoint one leader and will come up out of the land, for great will be the day of Jezreel. (Hosea 1:10–11)*

The fulfillment of God's promise to multiply Abraham's offspring was not limited to the nation of Israel. It is significant that Hosea's prophecy is cited in the New Testament in connection with the spread of the gospel to the Gentiles (Romans 9:25–26; 1 Peter 2:10). This means that "Abraham's offspring" includes not only those who are his physical descendants but also those who are of the faith of Abraham (Romans 4:16–17).

Numbers are more prominent in the New Testament than in the Old Testament. Jesus chose twelve apostles (Luke 6:13). After His ascension the believers in Jerusalem numbered approximately 120 (Acts 1:15). On the day of Pentecost three thousand more were added to the church (Acts 2:41). God continued to add new members on a daily basis until the size of the church grew to about five thousand (Acts 2:47; 4:4). Other passages in the book of Acts do not mention exact figures but describe the remarkable growth experienced by the early church (Acts 5:14; 6:1, 7; 9:31, 35, 42; 11:21, 24; 14:1, 21; 16:5; 17:12). Finally, the New Testament concludes with the apostle John's vision of heaven in which he saw 144,000 from all the tribes of Israel and "a great multitude that no one could count, from every nation, tribe, people and language, standing before the throne and in front of the Lamb. They were wearing white robes and were holding palm branches in their hands" (Revelation 7:4, 9).

Although these statements indicate that God is still at work multiplying His people, they do not focus on specific techniques or church growth strategies. Throughout the Bible numerical growth is seen as a by-product of divine blessing. Attendance figures, however important, are not the most important indicator of a church's spiritual health. It is possible for a church either to grow numerically for the wrong reasons or to shrink in size while doing the right things. For example, Jesus made statements during His ministry that seemed calculated to drive potential followers away because they were seeking Him with wrong motives (John 6:26–66). The death of Ananias and Sapphira after they tested God by lying to the Holy Spirit created such an atmosphere of healthy fear within the early church that those who were insincere did not attempt to join the believers (Acts 5:13).

It is not wrong for churches to want to increase in size. Nor should it be our goal to drive others away. We should pray, plan, and work for growth. In the end, however, the results lie with God. As we roll out the welcome mat for others in the congregation, we need to make certain in the process that we do not forget to welcome God.

Lord, make me more aware of Your presence as Your people gather for worship this Sunday. Show me how to make You welcome with my prayers, praise, and songs. Amen.

9

THE LORD'S COMMUNITY

> Why did you bring the Lord's community
> into this desert, that we and our livestock
> should die here? *(Numbers 20:4)*

The first week we lived in the small town where I served as pastor, my wife and I decided to take a walk down Main Street. We immediately noticed a difference from the large suburban communities in which we had lived previously. When we passed strangers on the street they nodded their heads and said hello to us. The drivers of oncoming cars gave a little wave as they came into view. Everybody seemed to know everybody else. Then we passed a little girl standing in her front yard near her mother. Wide-eyed, she began to back away as we drew nearer. "Mommy," she said in amazement, "I don't know them."

The word "community" immediately brings to mind images of friendliness and intimacy. We expect a community to be like a family whose members are bound together by close ties and are committed to one another in love. Sadly, the reality is often quite different. Although the people in our small town gave the appearance of being friendly, they were often cold to outsiders. When I sat down at the farmers' table in the local diner, the animated conversation that was going on before my arrival usually stopped. Long-term residents of the community sometimes complained, "I used to know everybody in town. Now I don't even know my neighbors."

God's people can experience similar difficulties. In many cases the greatest threat to their sense of community comes as a result of conflict. This is not a new problem. Moses and Aaron often had to deal with congregational conflict in their ministry. Usually the root problem for the conflict could be traced to unmet expectations. One of the most tragic examples of this occurred while the Israelites were encamped at Kadesh in the wilderness of Zin. On the surface it appeared to the people that Moses and Aaron had led them to a dead end. First Miriam died, and then the water ran out. Instead of praying that God would supply their need, the Israelites called a meeting to complain to Moses. This quickly escalated to a full-blown quarrel.

It began with a rash wish. The people confronted Moses and Aaron and said: "If only we had died when our brothers fell dead before the Lord!" (Numbers 20:3). The complainers felt that they would be better off dead. Ironically, with their next breath they accused Moses and Aaron of trying to kill them: "Why did you bring the Lord's community into this desert, that we and our livestock should die here? Why did you bring us up out of Egypt to this terrible place? It has no grain or figs, grapevines or pomegranates. And there is no water to drink!" (Numbers 20:4–5).

In yet another irony, they blamed Moses for doing the very thing that they had begged God to do for generations. They had prayed for deliverance from Egyptian slavery. Yet almost from the day that God answered that prayer they began to look wistfully back at their former life with a nostalgia that obscured all its pain and suffering (Exodus 16:3).

This is a common mistake. The past is often a poor gauge by which to judge the present. Compared to the present, the pleasures of the past usually seem enhanced, while the pain of earlier suffering is blunted. Selective memory transforms the "bad old days" into the "good old days."

Israel's complaint also ignored the fact that, although Moses and Aaron were Israel's human leaders, they were not really the ones leading Israel. God Himself had charted the course for their journey through the wilderness. The supernatural guidance of the cloud that went before them represented God's presence (Exodus 14:19; 32:34). Their complaint also overlooked the fact that they had not arrived at their final destination. The wilderness of Kadesh was a barren desert, but they had not yet reached the land "flowing with milk and honey" to which God had promised to bring them (Exodus 3:8). Moreover, God had given them an opportunity to enter the land earlier, but the people had balked when they learned that there were giants living in Canaan. Their refusal to take the land as God had commanded meant that Israel's entrance into Canaan would be delayed until the entire generation that came out of Egypt perished in the wilderness (Numbers 14:1–25). They blamed Moses and Aaron, but it was really their own lack of faith that had brought them to this place.

Israel's fight with Moses and Aaron was really an argument with God. It reflected an attempt to replace God's plan with Israel's own personal agenda. The Israelites had faced similar circumstances and God had provided exactly what was needed at the time (Exodus 17:1–7). He had provided food and water throughout their journey, often from a miraculous source. They were not satisfied with this. They wanted to determine what their circumstances would be like. The corrective to their false perspective was really hidden in their own words. This was the Lord's community. He had not abandoned them, even when they were at their worst. He was leading them along a predetermined path. True, it was not always as comfortable as they would have liked, but God had always provided for them, even in the midst of their greatest adversity.

Unfortunately, the Israelites were not the only ones who lost sight of God's authority on that day. Moses and Aaron acted just as rashly. Ordered only to speak to a rock, through which God would provide life-giving water, Moses took the rod that symbolized his authority and struck the rock instead: "He and Aaron gathered the assembly together in front of the rock and Moses said to them, 'Listen, you rebels, must we bring you water out of this rock?' Then Moses raised his arm and struck the rock twice with his staff. Water gushed out, and the community and their livestock drank" (Numbers 20:10–11). It was a decision that Moses and Aaron would regret until the end of their days. God decreed that neither of them would be allowed to lead Israel into the Land of Promise because they had failed to trust Him and publicly honor Him as holy (Numbers 20:12).

The fact that we live in community is no guarantee against destructive conflicts. Congregations and leaders alike can lose sight of the fact that the church is really the Lord's community. Members often have unrealistic expectations of their leaders and blame them for circumstances of their own making. Leaders, on the other hand, can be quick to lose patience and feel personally slighted when God's people are slow to respond to their suggestions. Both can be hurt in the process. It is only when we remember that God is the purpose for our coming together that we reflect His holiness in our community.

Lord of the Church, enable me to be sensitive to Your voice and quick to respond to the prompting of Your Holy Spirit. Rule in my life and in my church. Protect us from hurtful conflicts. Amen.

10

THE CHILDREN OF THE LORD

You are the children of the Lord your God.
Do not cut yourselves or shave the front of
your heads for the dead, for you are a people
holy to the Lord your God. Out of all the
peoples on the face of the earth, the Lord has
chosen you to be his treasured possession.
(*Deuteronomy 14:1–2*)

Samuel and Elmer were alike in many ways. They
were both in their eighties when I knew them.
Each had experienced the tragic loss of a child:
Elmer, when he lost his daughter to cancer, and
Samuel, when his daughter was struck and killed
by an automobile. Both men also liked to talk about
the past. Whenever I visited Samuel he told me stories about his years as a rural pastor and later as a
missionary to Japan. Elmer told me about his experiences growing up in a small town. He especially
enjoyed describing what it was like to run the old
steam-powered threshing machines that the farmers had used when he was a boy. Samuel and Elmer
were both troubled by declining health.

Despite their similarities, these two men differed radically in one important respect. When
Samuel talked about death, he did so with an air of
expectation. He reminisced about those who had
gone on before him as if they had just stepped out
of the room and were expected to return at any moment. He looked forward to his own death with the
anticipation of one who is planning a long-awaited

trip. Elmer, on the other hand, could not help choking up with despair whenever he talked about deceased friends and family members. He too looked forward to his own death, but only because he had grown weary of living. Samuel viewed death as the beginning of a new life. Elmer gave me the impression that it was the hopeless end to a disappointing existence.

The difference between these two men was a matter of faith rather than personality. Samuel's attitude about death was a reflection of his confidence in God. It is this kind of confidence that God urged His Old Testament people to have in Deuteronomy 14:1–2. The practices of lacerating oneself and shaving the front of one's head were mourning rituals commonly observed by Israel's neighbors. They reflected the stories of pagan mythology and were attempts to manipulate the deities for whom they were performed. Such practices were prohibited in Israel because they were associated with idolatrous worship.

More important, however, they were forbidden because such practices would deny Israel's unique relationship with God. The Israelites were told not to follow the mourning customs of the surrounding nations because: "You are the children of the Lord your God." This status was not earned but was bestowed upon them by God Himself. He had chosen them out of all the peoples on the earth. This made them God's own treasure, a precious possession belonging to Him alone. Pagan mourning rites did not reflect this. They implied that the gods had little interest in their worshipers and would only act on their behalf when compelled to do so by elaborate ceremonies designed to attract the gods' attention or appease their anger.

Israel's God, on the other hand, was to be viewed as a loving Father who had initiated the relationship with His people. He had adopted them as His own children and had promised to care for them. This unusual relationship set Israel apart from its neighbors. They were "holy" in the sense that they had been set apart by God and for God. This relationship was to be the basis for their obedience to God in life and their confidence in Him at the time of death.

Later in their history, Israel would need to be reminded of this important truth once again when they began to practice a different kind of mourning. After the initial enthusiasm of their return to the land of Palestine and the reconstruction of the second temple had worn off, the people began to wonder whether it was worthwhile to serve God. Outwardly they appeared to be worshiping God with zeal: fasting, praying, and offering sacrifices. God, however, seemed unresponsive, and the people began to complain: "It is futile to serve God. What did we gain by carrying out his requirements and going about like mourners before the Lord Almighty?" (Malachi 3:14). The solution would have been to shift the weight of their confidence from their religious rituals to heartfelt trust. Those whose fear of the Lord was genuine were assured that God had noticed: " 'They will be mine,' says the Lord Almighty, 'in the day when I make up my treasured possession. I will spare them, just as in compassion a man spares his son who serves him' " (Malachi 3:17).

Similar language is used of those of us who have trusted in Jesus Christ. Like Israel, we are God's treasured possession (Titus 2:14; 1 Peter 2:9). God's grace has made us children of the living God (Galatians 4:5–7). However, those of us who belong to Christ have a distinct advantage over God's Old Testament people. In addition to the objective testimony of Scripture that we belong to God, believers also have the immediate testimony of the Holy Spirit. The Holy Spirit is called "the spirit of adoption," and He provides personal assurance that we are the children of God (Romans 8:14–16).

It was this assurance that enabled my friend Samuel to be so confident in the face of death. Although he experienced grief at the death of others, it was a grief tempered by hope (1 Thessalonians 4:13). His lifetime of service to the Lord reflected the gratitude he felt for salvation in Christ and was not an attempt to trade personal sacrifice for divine favors. Samuel's awareness of God's love drove away the terrors of death and enabled him to meet it as a friend who would usher him into the presence of Christ and reunite him with others who had gone before.

Heavenly Father, thank You for making me Your precious possession. Give me such an assurance of Your love that when my own death comes, I will embrace it as a friend whose mission is to lead me into Your presence. In the words of the hymn writer: "Teach me to live that I may dread/ The grave as little as my bed." Amen.

11

CALLED BY THE NAME OF THE LORD

> The Lord will establish you as his holy
> people, as he promised you on oath, if you
> keep the commands of the Lord your God
> and walk in his ways. Then all the peoples
> on earth will see that you are called by the
> name of the Lord, and they will fear you.
> (*Deuteronomy 28:9–10*)

When my wife, Jane, was a little girl, her father
taught her to write her name as neatly as possible. "Your name is important," he explained. "It
tells people who you are." God's people were also
urged to be careful about their signature. For them,
however, their signature was not an impression
made by hand but one of actions. Israel's behavior
among the Gentile nations left behind a kind of living signature that identified them as God's own
people. God had promised to establish Israel as His
holy people and had sealed this promise with an
oath. The text does not say when this oath was giv-
en, but it is likely that it refers to the promises
made by God to Abraham that his descendants
would be as numerous as the sand on the seashore
and would possess the cities of their enemies (Genesis 22:15–17).

These promises brought with them obligations
that were later revealed in God's law. Obedience
brought blessing (Deuteronomy 28:1–14). Disobedience brought a curse (Deuteronomy 28:15–68).
These promises and threats must be understood

with the warning of Deuteronomy 9:5–6 as a back-
ground. There God reminded Israel that possession
of the land of Canaan was not something to be
earned:

> *It is not because of your righteousness or your integrity*
> *that you are going in to take possession of their land; but*
> *on account of the wickedness of these nations, the Lord*
> *your God will drive them out before you, to accomplish*
> *what he swore to your fathers, to Abraham, Isaac and*
> *Jacob. Understand, then, that it is not because of your*
> *righteousness that the Lord your God is giving you this*
> *good land to possess, for you are a stiff-necked people.*
> *(Deuteronomy 9:5–6)*

Israel's efforts could not earn God's favor. Their
status as God's chosen people was a gift of grace.
Grace and responsibility are not incompatible.
God's grace always brings with it an obligation to
obey His commands. Whereas we are saved by
grace through faith in Christ and not by works,
many of the blessings of the Christian life are contingent upon our obedience.

The commands of the Law were a concrete reflection of God's nature. Those who obeyed them
walked in His ways and left behind a divine imprint
that enabled others to know what God was really
like. On the other hand, when they disobeyed these
commands, they left others with a distorted view of
God. Like David, the great king of Israel who committed adultery, their disobedience was a kind of
blasphemy (2 Samuel 12:14).

God promised to "establish" Israel. This Hebrew term literally meant "to cause someone to

stand." Elsewhere this word is used in connection with Yahweh's covenant with Israel (Exodus 6:4). In Deuteronomy 28:9–10 it refers to Israel's experience of the blessings connected with this covenant. As the surrounding nations saw Israel blessed by God, they would know that He had singled them out to be His people. Literally, the Hebrew text says that the nations would know "that the name of Yahweh is proclaimed upon you."

This is the language of adoption. Jacob used similar terminology when he adopted Joseph's sons Ephraim and Manasseh (Genesis 48:16). It is also the language of blessing. In Numbers 6:27, the Lord told Moses that when the sons of Aaron pronounced the priestly blessing over God's people in public worship "they will put my name on the Israelites, and I will bless them." God's name symbolized His presence.

When the Lord appeared to Solomon a second time at Gibeon, He promised to answer Solomon's prayer to bless the temple in Jerusalem: "The Lord said to him: 'I have heard the prayer and plea you have made before me; I have consecrated this temple, which you have built, by putting my Name there forever. My eyes and my heart will always be there' " (1 Kings 9:3).

God's promise to pronounce His name over His people takes on special significance in the New Testament. In the Old Testament God promised that He would one day call the Gentiles by His name just as He had done for Israel (Amos 9:11–12). The New Testament reveals that this was to take place through the gospel of Christ (Acts 15:14–17). It is in the New Testament that we also learn that Jesus

Christ is the only name given under heaven by which we can be saved (Acts 4:12). All believers are adopted into God's family under the authority of the name of Christ (John 1:12–13). The name of Jesus is the source of all the Christian's blessings. Believers are baptized in His name (Acts 2:38; 8:12; 10:48). The gospel is preached in the name of Jesus (Acts 9:27–28). Forgiveness of sins and answers to prayer come through His name (Acts 10:43; John 16:24). Those who live in the New Jerusalem will have His name written on their foreheads as a symbol of God's presence (Revelation 22:4–5).

Because we are so closely identified with the name of Christ, we have a responsibility to guard our behavior. Irresponsible actions by believers can cause the name of Christ and the message of the gospel to be slandered (1 Timothy 6:1). It is not only our personal reputation and that of our church that is at stake. Those who name Jesus as Lord also have Christ's reputation to uphold: "Nevertheless, God's solid foundation stands firm, sealed with this inscription: 'The Lord knows those who are his,' and 'Everyone who confesses the name of the Lord must turn away from wickedness'" (2 Timothy 2:19).

God of Israel, You have called me to be Your child and given me Your name. Help me to guard my actions today so that others will see in them an accurate reflection of Your character.

12
THE LORD'S ARMY

Now when Joshua was near Jericho, he looked up and saw a man standing in front of him with a drawn sword in his hand. Joshua went up to him and asked, "Are you for us or for our enemies?" "Neither," he replied, "but as commander of the army of the Lord I have now come." Then Joshua fell facedown to the ground in reverence, and asked him, "What message does my Lord have for his servant?" *(Joshua 5:13–14)*

Even a fool would be suspicious when stumbling upon a stranger with a drawn weapon on the eve of an important military campaign—and Joshua was no fool. He was no coward either. Joshua was a seasoned veteran of several key battles. He had led Israel to victory when they fought against the Amalekites at Rephidim (Exodus 17:9–13). He had defeated Sihon, the Amorite king who had refused to let Israel pass through his territory, and Og, the king of Bashan (Numbers 21:21–35). He was one of the two spies who really believed that God could defeat the giants of Canaan (Numbers 14:6–9). He had been Moses' chief assistant and was his designated successor (Numbers 27:15–20; Deuteronomy 1:38; Joshua 1:1–9). So when Joshua saw a man with a drawn sword in his hand, standing in his path during a reconnaissance mission outside the city of Jericho, he asked the obvious question. In effect, he said: "Whose side are you on?"

"Neither" was the surprising answer. "But as commander of the army of the Lord I have now come" (Joshua 5:14a). In view of all that Israel had experienced, this reply seems remarkable. Had not God already demonstrated that He was "for" Israel? He had chosen them out of all the nations. He had rescued them from slavery in Egypt and defeated Pharaoh's powerful army in the process. He had given them miraculous victories over their enemies during their journey through the wilderness. He had even promised them ultimate victory in their conquest of Canaan (Joshua 1:3–5). If God was not on Israel's side, whose side was He on?

Curiously, Joshua does not seem to have been disturbed by the answer he received to his question. Recognizing immediately that he was not dealing with an ordinary soldier but with the Lord, appearing to him in human form as the Angel of the Lord, Joshua bowed down in worship.

The Angel of the Lord appears numerous times in the Old Testament as God's messenger, but is often addressed as God Himself by those who encounter Him. For example, He appeared to Sarah's servant Hagar. After her meeting with the Angel of the Lord, Hagar declared "I have now seen the One who sees me," and gave the Lord the name "You are the God who sees me" (Genesis 16:13). Jacob wrestled with the Angel of the Lord while making the return trip from Haran to Canaan. He marveled, "I saw God face to face, and yet my life was spared" (Genesis 32:30). Many biblical scholars believe that the Angel of the Lord was really Jesus Christ appearing in human form prior to the Incarnation.

Joshua's lack of surprise at the Angel's response, and his spontaneous act of reverence, speak of a man who knew his place. Initially, he had addressed the Angel of the Lord as if He were a mere soldier. If this had been true, the stranger's course of action would have been plain. If he was Joshua's enemy, he must fight or deliver his message. If he was one of Joshua's soldiers or an ally, he must follow orders. However, once the stranger's true identity became known, Joshua's perspective reversed completely. Joshua was no longer the commander but the one being commanded.

This may explain why the Angel of the Lord responded to Joshua's question as He did. He had not come to serve Joshua's purposes or even those of Israel. He was not "for" Israel in that sense. Rather, Joshua and Israel had been called to serve His purposes. The Angel of the Lord revealed an unusual battle plan to Joshua. Instead of gaining the victory by sheer force, the strategy had worship at its center. The hosts of Israel were to march around Jericho in a solemn procession with the ark at the center and with trumpets sounding. They were to do this once a day for six days and then seven times on the seventh day: "When the trumpets sounded, the people shouted, and at the sound of the trumpet, when the people gave a loud shout, the wall collapsed; so every man charged straight in, and they took the city" (Joshua 6:20).

We have much to learn from Joshua's experience. Like him, we are under orders. Those who follow Jesus Christ are to practice the discipline required of a soldier: "Endure hardship with us like a good soldier of Christ Jesus. No one serving as a soldier gets involved in civilian affairs—he wants to please his commanding officer" (2 Timothy 2:3–4). It is tempting to try to enlist Christ's aid for our own pet projects. We can easily come to Him with our own plans and ask Him to bless them, without first seeking to know what His will is for our lives or churches.

It is essential that we remember that Jesus is our Master and Commander. Also, like Joshua, we are engaged in a conflict whose victory will depend upon a supernatural strategy: "For though we live in the world, we do not wage war as the world does. The weapons we fight with are not the weapons of the world. On the contrary, they have divine power to demolish strongholds" (2 Corinthians 10:3–4). How might it affect our churches if we saw worship as a means of waging battle against Satan's interests and furthering those of Christ? Finally, like Joshua, we have been assured ultimate victory. The day is coming when the Commander of the army of the Lord will return. With the church at His side, He will defeat His enemies and establish His kingdom (Revelation 19:11–20:6).

Master and Commander, forgive me for attempting to enlist Your aid in my own pet projects without first seeking to know Your will. Help me to remember that I am under orders and to set my hope on the ultimate victory that is assured in Christ. Amen.

13

THE HOUSE OF ISRAEL

Then the elders and all those at the gate said, "We are witnesses. May the Lord make the woman who is coming into your home like Rachel and Leah, who together built up the house of Israel. May you have standing in Ephrathah and be famous in Bethlehem. Through the offspring the Lord gives you by this young woman, may your family be like that of Perez, whom Tamar bore to Judah." (*Ruth 4:11–12*)

Someone has said that a house is just "a machine for living in." However, when the Bible uses the term, it often does not refer to the dwelling place, but to the people who dwell in it. The Hebrew term that is translated "house" can also mean "household." It was used in just such a sense in the blessing uttered by the elders who witnessed the marriage of Ruth the Moabitess to Boaz the farmer of Bethlehem. They said: "May the Lord make the woman who is coming into your home like Rachel and Leah, who together built up the house of Israel" (Ruth 4:11).

This prayer welcomed Ruth into the family of God's people. This was remarkable, in view of the fact that she was a foreigner. It seems even more remarkable when we consider that she was originally from the land of Moab. The people of Moab were distant relatives of the Israelites, the descendants of Lot through his eldest daughter (Genesis 19:37).

Despite this connection, the Moabites had refused to allow Israel to pass through their territory on the way to Canaan (Judges 11:14–17). Balak, one of their kings, had even hired the prophet Balaam to curse Israel (Numbers 22–24). When he was unsuccessful, Balaam taught the Moabites to use seductive techniques to introduce idolatrous worship into Israel (Numbers 25:1–9; 31:15–16; 2 Peter 2:14–16). Perhaps most striking of all is the fact that, according to the Law of Moses, Moabites were forbidden to enter the congregation of Israel: "No Ammonite or Moabite or any of his descendants may enter the assembly of the Lord, even down to the tenth generation" (Deuteronomy 23:3). Although it is untranslated in the *New International Version,* the Hebrew text adds the word "forever" at the end of this verse!

Some scholars believe that two different prohibitions are referred to in this verse, an exclusion of ten generations for the Moabites and a permanent exclusion for the Ammonites. Others see the two as synonymous, with the number ten used as a symbol for complete exclusion. In either case, it is clear that Ruth's inclusion into the household of Israel was a matter of grace. However, the favors bestowed on Ruth did not end there. Not only was she included in the family of Israel, she became the great-grandmother of David, Israel's greatest king (Ruth 4:17). She is also mentioned in the genealogy of Jesus (Matthew 1:5).

Ruth's acceptance as a part of the household of Israel foreshadowed the extension of God's grace to the Gentiles through the preaching of the gospel. Although the church is still a household, it is no longer identified with a single family. Instead of being the household of Israel, all those who trust in Jesus Christ become a part of "God's household" (1 Timothy 3:15). Prior to the coming of Christ, Israel's unique standing as God's chosen people had created a barrier for non-Jews. Exclusion from citizenship in Israel meant that most Gentiles would never have access to the promises of God, since they were not joined to Him in a covenant relationship (Ephesians 2:11–12).

A few Gentiles became proselytes of Judaism, but even these were usually treated as outsiders. Nowhere was this so vividly illustrated than in the temple, where a four-and-a-half foot dividing wall confined non-Jewish proselytes to the outer court. In the apostle Paul's day, signs were posted on this wall in Greek and Latin warning that any Gentile who passed beyond that point would be subject to death. But actually the death of Christ had already reconciled Jews and Gentiles:

> *For he himself is our peace, who has made the two one and has destroyed the barrier, the dividing wall of hostility, by abolishing in his flesh the law with its commandments and regulations. His purpose was to create in himself one new man out of the two, thus making peace, and in this one body to reconcile both of them to God through the cross. (Ephesians 2:14–16a)*

Elsewhere Paul compared this new creation to the grafting together of two types of olive trees. The new tree consists of the native root supporting "wild" branches that have been grafted in (Romans 11:17–19). However, this does not mean that God is finished with the House of Israel. On the contrary, one of God's purposes in extending the offer of the gospel to the Gentiles was to provoke Israel to spiritual jealousy and to help them see their need for Jesus Christ as their promised Messiah (Romans 11:11). The Scriptures promise that one day there will be a mass turning to Christ among the descendants of Abraham (Romans 11:25–27). Jesus Christ will return and establish His kingdom with its center at Jerusalem and fulfill God's promises to Israel.

Ruth's story is a reminder that God's purpose is to call to Himself a people made up of every tribe, tongue, and nation (Revelation 5:9). Because of this, our circle of interest should include those who are different from us. It is very possible that if we had been living in Ruth's day we would not have looked upon her as a likely candidate for conversion, let alone considered her a central figure in God's redemptive plan. There may be some that we are now overlooking because their past or their ancestry makes them seem just as unlikely. Others may escape our notice because we tend to stick to the company of people who are "like us." It is sobering to realize that if those who first preached the message of Christ had not overcome similar prejudices it is unlikely that we would now be saved.

God and Father, by Your grace I am now part of Your family. Use me to extend this invitation to others, especially to those who are different from me. Fulfill Your promises to the Household of Israel and bring them to faith in Christ. Amen.

14
THE VIRGIN DAUGHTER OF ZION

Then Isaiah son of Amoz sent a message
to Hezekiah: "This is what the Lord, the God
of Israel, says: I have heard your prayer
concerning Sennacherib king of Assyria.
This is the word that the Lord has spoken
against him: 'The Virgin Daughter of Zion
despises you and mocks you. The Daughter
of Jerusalem tosses her head as you flee.'"
(2 Kings 19:20–21)

There are many great cities in the world.
Jerusalem stands out from the rest because it is
the only city that God ever chose to claim as His
own. The Lord called Jerusalem "the city where I
chose to put my Name" (1 Kings 11:36). The title
most commonly used to refer to Jerusalem was
"Zion" or "the Daughter of Zion."

Zion was originally a Jebusite fortress captured
by David. Its name may come from a word that
meant "protect" or "defend." When David made it
his personal dwelling place it became known as
"the City of David" (2 Samuel 5:7). After he moved
the ark of the covenant to Zion it also became identified as God's dwelling place. According to the
prediction of Psalm 2:6, Israel's Messiah will one
day be enthroned in Zion. The Virgin Daughter of
Zion was "the joy of the whole earth" and "perfect
in beauty" (Psalm 48:2; 50:2; Lamentations 2:15).
Because of its importance, Zion's fortunes symbolized those of God's people as a whole. The eventual

fall of Jerusalem to the Babylonians in 586 B.C. was the final stroke in God's judgment of His people.

Because God manifested His presence in Zion, it was also the place God's people looked to for salvation. David prayed: "Oh, that salvation for Israel would come out of Zion! When the Lord restores the fortunes of his people, let Jacob rejoice and Israel be glad!" (Psalm 14:7; cf. Psalm 20:2). At the dedication of the temple in Jerusalem, Solomon, David's son and successor, prayed: "May your eyes be open toward this temple night and day, this place of which you said, 'My Name shall be there,' so that you will hear the prayer your servant prays toward this place. Hear the supplication of your servant and of your people Israel when they pray toward this place. Hear from heaven, your dwelling place, and when you hear, forgive" (1 Kings 8:29–30). God reigned in Zion, and those who worshiped there appeared before Him (Psalm 84:7).

It is not surprising, then, that King Hezekiah became distraught when the Assyrians besieged Jerusalem and urged its inhabitants to desert the city. While the military threat was grave, the spiritual insult was even worse. The Assyrian commander taunted those who watched from the city walls: "Where are the gods of Hamath and Arpad? Where are the gods of Sepharvaim, Hena and Ivvah? Have they rescued Samaria from my hand? Who of all the gods of these countries has been able to save his land from me? How then can the Lord deliver Jerusalem from my hand?" (2 Kings 18:34–35).

Hezekiah did not respond with a display of military power. Instead, he took the contemptuous message sent by the Assyrian commander and spread it out in the presence of the Lord (2 Kings 19:14–19). Interestingly, the appeal of his prayer was not based upon the sanctity of the city of Jerusalem but upon God's own reputation. The Assyrians' insult had placed Hezekiah's God in the same category as the powerless idols of the Gentiles. It had even implied that Yahweh was behind Assyria's successful military campaigns (2 Kings 18:25). This was partially true. The Lord had described Assyria as "the rod of my anger" and said of them that they were the ones "in whose hand is the club of my wrath." However, He had also promised that once He had finished chastening Jerusalem, He would "punish the king of Assyria for the willful pride of his heart and the haughty look in his eyes" (Isaiah 10:5, 12).

The Lord answered Hezekiah swiftly. The night after Hezekiah's prayer, the Angel of the Lord went through the Assyrian camp and put to death 185,000 men (2 Kings 19:35). Although correct in assuming that they were tools in the hands of the God of Israel and Judah, the Assyrians had failed to understand that they were also accountable to Him for their actions.

However, if this was true of Gentiles, how much more would it be true of God's people? The fact that the Lord had protected "the Virgin Daughter of Zion" from Assyrian aggression did not guarantee its future safety. A century later the Babylonians posed a similar threat to Jerusalem. This time, however, the Lord did not protect the city. The prophet Jeremiah, who witnessed the destruction firsthand, lamented that Jerusalem had "suffered a grievous wound, a crushing blow" (Jeremiah 14:17).

He also complained: "The Lord has rejected all the warriors in my midst; he has summoned an army against me to crush my young men. In his wine-press the Lord has trampled the Virgin Daughter of Judah" (Lamentations 1:15).

The Lord's protection of Jerusalem under Hezekiah's reign should have led God's people to faith and obedience. Instead, it revealed an unhealthy spiritual complacency that would eventually lead to the destruction of Jerusalem. This became evident when Hezekiah's pride led him to show his riches to Babylonian emissaries that had been sent to congratulate him on his miraculous recovery from a near fatal illness. After Hezekiah showed the envoys his storehouses and his armory, the Lord sent Isaiah the prophet to tell Hezekiah that the time would come when all that he had shown them would be carried off to distant Babylon. Instead of grieving over this eventuality, Hezekiah rejoiced that there would be peace in his own lifetime (2 Kings 20:12–19).

Hezekiah's successors, for the most part, were given to idolatry. His son Manasseh took a carved pole dedicated to the Assyrian fertility goddess Asherah and put it in the temple (2 Kings 21:7). Amon worshiped the idols of his father Manasseh (vv. 20–22). Although there was a significant revival under Josiah, his reforms were not able to halt the inevitable judgment that had been promised for Jerusalem (2 Kings 23:26–27). Josiah's son followed the evil example of his ancestors, as did the remainder of those who ruled in Jerusalem (vv. 31–32, 36–37; 24:8–9).

The line that separates confidence from complacency in the believer's life is easily seen. Confidence leads to a greater sense of dependency upon God. Complacency leads to dependency upon one's own resources. The apostle Paul was supremely confident, but never in a smug, self-satisfied way. He was certain that God had equipped him to be competent in ministry, but he did not rely upon his own ability or training (2 Corinthians 3:6; Philippians 3:3–7). He also recognized that every believer will be asked to give an account to God (Romans 14:12). Confidence in God did not remove from him the responsibility to strive for excellence in his service to Christ (Philippians 3:13–14).

Father of Mercy, help me not to allow Your goodness to lead to complacency in my life. Examine my heart by Your Spirit and bring to light those things that are displeasing to You. Amen.

15

THE PRIDE OF JACOB

How awesome is the Lord Most High, the great King over all the earth! He subdued nations under us, peoples under our feet. He chose our inheritance for us, the pride of Jacob, whom he loved. *(Psalm 47:2–4)*

Like the name we studied in the previous chapter, this title does not refer to the people of Israel but refers to the land in which they lived. God's promised blessings to Israel were both material and spiritual. The Hebrew term that is translated "inheritance" literally referred to property. The Lord had commanded Abraham to leave Haran where he had been living with his family and to "go to the land I will show you" (Genesis 12:1). He had promised to create a great nation from Abraham's offspring and to make him a blessing to all the peoples on earth. He had also promised to give Abraham's descendants the land of Canaan (Genesis 12:7). Later, this promise was repeated when Abraham entered into a covenant of faith with the Lord and was reckoned as righteous (Genesis 15:6–19). There the Lord described the scope of Abraham's inheritance as being: "from the river of Egypt to the great river, the Euphrates—the land of the Kenites, Kenizzites, Kadmonites, Hittites, Perizzites, Rephaites, Amorites, Canaanites, Girgashites and Jebusites" (vv. 18b–21).

The fact that God promised to give Abraham and his descendants land that was already inhabited by others may seem unfair. As Creator, however, the ultimate right of ownership over all property belongs to Him. He is not merely ruler over Israel but "the great King over all the earth." As such He exercises sovereign authority, even over those who do not recognize Him as Lord. One aspect of this authority is the right to assign a nation's location as its dwelling place. This has not been done arbitrarily. According to the apostle Paul, God's ultimate purpose is redemptive in nature: "From one man he made every nation of men, that they should inhabit the whole earth; and he determined the times set for them and the exact places where they should live. God did this so that men would seek him and perhaps reach out for him and find him, though he is not far from each one of us" (Acts 17:26–27).

Where Canaan was concerned, behavior was also a factor. Although God promised to give the land to Abraham, his descendants were not allowed to enter Canaan for approximately four hundred years because the sin of the inhabitants of Palestine had not reached its full measure (Genesis 15:16). Later, when Joshua finally led the armies of Israel into Canaan to drive out its inhabitants, the Lord reminded him that the nations were being dispossessed because of their own wickedness (Deuteronomy 9:4–6).

God gave Israel the land but retained ultimate ownership of it. For this reason property could be sold by those who were in economic distress but not sold permanently (Leviticus 25:23). Purchasers gained only the right of temporary use. In the Year of Jubilee all property was to return to the families to whom it had originally been assigned. Even prior

to the Year of Jubilee a kinsman retained the right
to repurchase the land (Leviticus 25:25–28). Fur-
thermore, although the land belonged to Israel as
an inheritance, this did not automatically guarantee
them a permanent residency there. The same God
who had promised unparalleled blessings for their
obedience also warned the Israelites that their disobedience would lead to expulsion from the Land
of Promise (Deuteronomy 4:27; 28:36–37). Eventually, Israel's persistent idolatry forced God to
exercise His authority as divine landlord and drive
them from the land (2 Kings 17:6; 25:1–12).

Fortunately, the same curses that had warned
of this eventuality also included a promise that
God's people would be restored to their inheritance
if they repented:

> *When all these blessings and curses I have set before you*
> *come upon you and you take them to heart wherever the*
> *Lord your God disperses you among the nations, and*
> *when you and your children return to the Lord your*
> *God and obey him with all your heart and with all your*
> *soul according to everything I command you today, then*
> *the Lord your God will restore your fortunes and have*
> *compassion on you and gather you again from all the*
> *nations where he scattered you. (Deuteronomy 30:1–3)*

Abraham, Isaac, and Jacob did not possess
Canaan during their lifetimes. Instead, they lived
there as though they were aliens in a foreign country (Hebrews 11:8–9, 13). Moreover, although God
gave Israel an opportunity to possess all of Canaan,
portions of the land remained unconquered after
the death of Joshua (Judges 1:19, 21, 27, 29–34;

3:1–4). Some promises related to the land have yet to be fulfilled. All God's purposes for the Land of Promise will finally be accomplished when Jesus returns to establish His kingdom. He will reign from Jerusalem as Israel's Messiah for one thousand years (Revelation 20:1–6).

God's promises should be the object of the believer's hope. Those referred to in the text are called "the pride of Jacob." Although the Bible frequently speaks of pride in negative terms, pride can be a good thing when it is properly focused. For example, we are told to take pride in our knowledge of God (Jeremiah 9:24). We can experience an appropriate form of pride when we see the work that God is doing in others (2 Corinthians 12:5). We can even take a certain amount of pride in our weaknesses when they underscore God's strength and show others how He has enabled us to serve Him (2 Corinthians 12:9–10). The pride that we experience should not be rooted in arrogance, since God's promises to us are not based upon our own personal merit. The promises celebrated by the psalmist sprang from God's love for His people. They were undeserved. The same is true of the blessings we experience in Christ. They are the result of God's grace. In the end, God's promises have very little to say about us. Rather, they tell us a great deal about the One who made them and who keeps them.

Lord Most High, I acknowledge You today, not only as King over all the earth, but as King of my life. Open my eyes to the promises You have made to me in Your Word so that I may depend on You more. Amen.

16
MY CONSECRATED ONES

> Our God comes and will not be silent; a fire devours before him, and around him a tempest rages. He summons the heavens above, and the earth, that he may judge his people: "Gather to me my consecrated ones, who made a covenant with me by sacrifice." *(Psalm 50:3–5)*

Could you stand to be in the same room with God? On the surface, the answer seems obvious. The Bible, especially the book of Psalms, is filled with the statements of those who express their longing for God's presence. David expected to be filled with joy and to experience eternal pleasures in God's presence (Psalm 16:11). He thought of the presence of God as a place of safety (Psalm 31:20). Even after David sinned he begged God not to cast him away from His presence (Psalm 51:11).

Asaph, the leader of choral worship under King David and the author of Psalm 50, offered another perspective. He compared God's presence to a roaring fire that consumes everything in its path. Moses used a similar metaphor to describe God, associating it with His jealousy: "Be careful not to forget the covenant of the Lord your God that he made with you; do not make for yourselves an idol in the form of anything the Lord your God has forbidden. For the Lord your God is a consuming fire, a jealous God" (Deuteronomy 4:23–24). Moses also employed this metaphor to describe God's ability to destroy Israel's enemies in Canaan. He promised that the Lord would go before His people "like a devouring fire" to subdue, destroy, drive out the nations already living there (Deuteronomy 9:1–3).

Fire was often a feature on those occasions when God made Himself known to men and women. The Lord first appeared to Moses in a burning bush (Exodus 3:2). During the Exodus and Israel's subsequent journey through the wilderness, pillars of smoke and fire visibly reassured God's people of His presence and protected them from their enemies (Exodus 13:21–22). When the Law was given to Moses, the Lord descended upon Mount Sinai in smoke and fire (Exodus 24:17). On a few occasions God showed His acceptance of offerings made to Him by consuming them with fire that came out from His presence (Judges 6:21; 1 Kings 18:38). He also used fire to judge those who had sinned (Genesis 19:24; Leviticus 10:1–2; Numbers 16:35).

In addition, Asaph compared God's presence to a raging tempest. When the rebellious prophet Jonah tried to outrun the presence of God, the Lord signaled His pursuit with a storm so violent that the ship Jonah was sleeping in threatened to break into pieces (Jonah 1:4).

However, the most terrifying aspect of Asaph's description of the Lord's presence was not the phenomena that accompanied it but the purpose for it: "He summons the heavens above, and the earth, that he may judge his people" (Psalm 50:4). In His presence, all that God's people had offered came under scrutiny. Under this evaluation a critical flaw was revealed. The problem was not with the

offerings so much as with the motivation behind
them. Israel had begun to view sacrifice and offering as a kind of spiritual bribe. They had fallen
into a pagan mind-set, which assumed that God
could be appeased by religious ritual regardless of
the worshipers' inner condition. The Lord corrected
this false assumption by pointing out that He derived no personal benefit from Israel's offerings: "I
have no need of a bull from your stall or of goats
from your pens, for every animal of the forest is
mine, and the cattle on a thousand hills" (Psalm
50:9–10).

Sacrifice, although important, could never substitute for true holiness. Because of this, the Lord's
call to worship in this psalm was addressed to His
"consecrated ones." This term came from the Hebrew word for "faithful." It could also be translated
"pious" or "godly," and it referred to those who put
their faith into practice. Consequently, the criticism
in this psalm was directed at those who ignored the
instruction of God's word and followed the example of the wicked (Psalm 50:16–17). Despite all the
show of their religious practices, their true character
was evident by their actions and more importantly
by their words (Psalm 50:19–20).

Similar concerns are expressed in the New Testament. James taught that true faith must be
reflected in action and that faith without works is
dead (James 2:14–26). He also warned that a reli-
gion that does not affect one's tongue is worthless
(James 1:26). The apostle Paul reminded the Colossians that believers' words and deeds are both
essential components of their testimony: "Be wise in
the way you act toward outsiders; make the most of

every opportunity. Let your conversation be always full of grace, seasoned with salt, so that you may know how to answer everyone" (Colossians 4:5–6).

The biblical word that summarizes these characteristics is "holiness." In the Christian life holiness is both a practice and a gift. It is a practice in the sense that the transforming work of Christ is to be reflected in our daily actions. We are to "make every effort to live in peace with all men and to be holy; without holiness no one will see the Lord" (Hebrews 12:14). It is a gift in the sense that the believer's holiness comes from Christ. His death and resurrection have purchased a righteous standing for all those who believe in Him. The empowerment of His Spirit transforms us so that we are able to put aside old behaviors and exchange them for new ones (Ephesians 4:22–24; Colossians 3:8–10). As a result, we can look forward to the time that we will stand before Him in judgment (Philippians 3:8–9).

Apart from the work of Christ we would not want to experience God's presence. Indeed, we could not even bear it. However, once we have experienced the grace of God by placing our faith in Jesus, the prospect of being with Christ is even better than life itself (Philippians 1:23).

Holy Lord, I hear Your call to worship. Help me to set aside those practices that reflect the old nature and to be transformed by Your Holy Spirit, so that I might truly be one of Your "Consecrated Ones." Through Christ I long to experience Your presence today in fresh ways. Amen.

17

GOD'S DOVE

> Do not hand over the life of your dove to wild beasts; do not forget the lives of your afflicted people forever. *(Psalm 74:19)*

Lovers often use nicknames to refer to each other. When my parents were dating they called each other "Bill" and "Coo." My wife sometimes refers to me as "Johnny." Parents also use nicknames as a sign of affection. A father might call his son "Buddy" or his daughter "Princess." In Psalm 74:19 the psalmist uses the affectionate nickname "your dove" to refer to Israel. This Hebrew term referred specifically to the turtledove. In the Law, turtledoves were offered in sacrifice and were frequently used in purification rituals (Leviticus 1:14; 5:7, 11; 12:6, 8; 14:22, 30). Solomon, using a more general Hebrew word, described the dove as a symbol of love and beauty (Song of Songs 1:15; 2:14; 4:1). After he had recovered from a life-threatening illness, King Hezekiah said that he had "moaned like a mourning dove" (Isaiah 38:14).

The author of Psalm 74 characterized the nation of Israel as a dove to emphasize God's love for His people and to underscore their vulnerability. The psalm itself was prompted by the writer's awareness of the terrible sufferings experienced by the nation. Although the psalm is ascribed to Asaph, a contemporary of David, the circumstances described in it seem more consistent with the inva-

sion of Jerusalem by Babylonians (586 B.C.). It is
possible that the psalm was originally a prophecy of
a destruction that was to come later. In 2 Chronicles 29:30, Asaph is called a "seer," another word
for prophet (Isaiah 30:9–10). Some, however, have
suggested that the ascription actually refers to one
of Asaph's descendants (cf. Ezra 3:10 and Nehemiah 11:22).

The psalm opens with a plaintive cry: "Why
have you rejected us forever, O God? Why does
your anger smolder against the sheep of your pasture?" (Psalm 74:1). From the psalmist's perspective,
it appeared as if God had forgotten His covenant
with Israel. How could this not be true, when the
temple was in ruins and its sanctuary overrun by
the enemy (Psalm 74:3–8)? Prior to the destruction
of Jerusalem, the regard of God's people for the
temple had grown to superstitious proportions.
They looked upon it as a talisman strong enough to
protect the city's inhabitants from its enemies, regardless of their own actions. However, the
prophets repeatedly warned that without true re-
pentance Jerusalem was doomed (Jeremiah 7:3–8).

As troubling as these calamities were, the worst
blow was yet to come. God Himself was to become
silent. For centuries the prophets had instructed,
warned, and encouraged God's people, but to no
avail. In time even their voice would cease to be
heard: "We are given no miraculous signs; no
prophets are left, and none of us knows how long
this will be" (Psalm 74:9). For generations God had
shouted while His rebellious people blocked their
ears in defiance. In the silence that followed they
begged Him for the faintest whisper.

God's grace should not tempt us to act presumptuously toward Him. Those who ignore His warnings will bear the consequences. It is true that if we have placed our faith in Jesus Christ we will never be condemned, but we may suffer from lasting scars left behind by sinful choices. Our resistance to conviction may silence the prompting of the Holy Spirit (1 Thessalonians 5:19). The dynamic of grace assures us of our standing in Christ but does not make us immune from divine chastening. On the contrary, it guarantees it (Hebrews 12:4–13).

In his appeal the psalm writer focused on three aspects of God's relationship with His people. He began by appealing to God as ruler (Psalm 74:12a). When the Babylonians finally sacked Jerusalem, they captured Judah's king and carried him off into exile (2 Kings 25:4–7; Lamentations 2:9). Although His people no longer had an earthly king, God continued to govern their affairs. Like the psalmist, we too can be confident that God's control in our lives is not contingent upon the nature of our problems. In the very worst of circumstances, He continues to govern our lives. God can even turn the sinful actions of unbelievers so that they serve His own loving purposes (Habakkuk 1:6–11).

Second, the psalm writer appealed to God as Savior, beginning with the deliverance of Israel at the Red Sea: "It was you who split open the sea by your power; you broke the heads of the monster in the waters. It was you who crushed the heads of Leviathan and gave him as food to the creatures of the desert" (Psalm 74:13–14). The Hebrew term that is translated "Leviathan" is used elsewhere in Scripture to refer to a large seagoing animal, possi-

bly a crocodile or even a sea monster (Job 41:1;
Psalm 104:26; Isaiah 27:1). In this psalm the term
is used as a symbol of the Egyptian armies. The
gruesome picture of the bodies of the Egyptian
army scattered along the banks of the Nile as "food
to the creatures of the desert" provided a needed reminder of God's ability to defeat His enemies. God
also acted as Israel's savior by providing for their
needs during the journey through the wilderness.
He had "opened up springs and streams" by sup-
plying water in the desert, while drying up "the
ever flowing rivers" and allowing His people to
cross the Red Sea and the Jordan (Exodus 17:6;
Joshua 2:10).

Third, the psalmist appealed to God as Creator.
The fact that the God of Israel was also the One who
had created the sun and moon, fixed the boundaries
of the earth, and set the cycle of the seasons in mo-
tion underscored His unlimited resources of power
(Psalm 74:16–17). Those who were taken captive by
their enemies and carried to lands that did not worship the same God would not be beyond the reach
of His power. The whole earth was His.

Based upon this, the author made several requests (Psalm 74:18–23). The first was to ask God
to remember how the enemy had mocked and re-
viled Yahweh's name. Although there was no
ground for an appeal based upon merit, he could
appeal for help on the basis of God's own glory. The
psalm writer asked for protection and compared
the circumstances of God's people to that of a help-
less dove in danger of being devoured by wild
beasts. He also pleaded with God, "Have regard for
your covenant" (Psalm 74:20). The Hebrew text

pictures someone taking a long and careful look at
something. In effect, the psalmist appealed to God
to look, not at Israel's sins, but at His own covenant
promises. This was the same approach taken by
Moses when he made intercession for Israel after
their sin with the golden calf (Exodus 32:11–13).
Viewing his circumstances from this perspective
gave Asaph the courage to call upon God to defend
Israel and defeat His enemies.

When we disappoint God, we tend to focus on
our sin. His focus is upon the promises He has
made on our behalf. He will not ignore our sin but
will deal with it appropriately, providing instruction and chastening where necessary. He may even
allow us to experience temporary consequences in
this life because of it. But it will not brand us forever. We will always be His.

*God of Grace and Mercy, forgive me for the times I
have fallen short of Your standard. Thank You for the
evidence that I see of Your loving discipline in my life today. Use my circumstances to bring glory to Your name
and mold me into the image of Your Son. Amen.*

18
SODOM AND GOMORRAH

> Hear the word of the Lord, you rulers of Sodom; listen to the law of our God, you people of Gomorrah! "The multitude of your sacrifices—what are they to me?" says the Lord. "I have more than enough of burnt offerings, of rams and the fat of fattened animals; I have no pleasure in the blood of bulls and lambs and goats." *(Isaiah 1:10–11)*

The English poet John Dryden was once asked to act as judge in an impromptu poetry contest involving several influential friends. The first to be finished was the Earl of Dorset. Dryden took the composition from him and waited until the rest had completed their work before looking at it. When everyone was done, Dryden began to read through the works that had been submitted to him. The expression on his face showed that the contestants had taken their challenge seriously and that the final decision was bound to be a difficult one. However, when at last he came to the paper that the Earl of Dorset had given him, he smiled broadly and announced that he had found his winner. "I will have to award the prize to my Lord Dorset," he explained. He then showed the others what Dorset had written: "I promise to pay John Dryden, or order on demand the sum of £500. Dorset."

There are occasions when bribery can be a persuasive means of influencing those in authority. The writer of Proverbs noted: "A bribe is a charm to

the one who gives it; wherever he turns, he suc-
ceeds" (Proverbs 17:8). Some even felt that they
could bribe God through their sacrifices and offerings. Deluded into thinking that their observance
of the rituals prescribed by the Mosaic Law was
enough to make them righteous, they ignored
God's moral demands in their daily lives. The title
"Sodom and Gomorrah" was God's way of arresting
the attention of Israel and Judah and helping them
to see how sinful their actions truly were.

Sodom and Gomorrah were the two "cities of
the plain" that God destroyed by raining down
burning sulfur upon them (Genesis 19:23–29).
They were notorious for sexual sin, especially the
practice of homosexuality (Genesis 19:4–5). However, this was not the only sin of theirs that merited
divine judgment. The prophet Ezekiel condemned
Sodom for pride, materialism, and selfishness:
"Now this was the sin of your sister Sodom: She
and her daughters were arrogant, overfed and unconcerned; they did not help the poor and needy.
They were haughty and did detestable things before
me. Therefore I did away with them as you have
seen" (Ezekiel 16:49–50).

In the New Testament similar practices are also
listed along with the more obvious sins of sexual
immorality as acts of the sinful nature. Things like
hatred, discord, selfish ambition, and envy are giv-
en equal weight with sexual immorality, impurity,
debauchery, and idolatry (Galatians 5:19–21). This
perspective reflects that of Jesus, who did not limit
sin to action alone but ultimately traced it to the
hidden attitude of the heart. He warned that the act
of adultery could ultimately be traced to a lustful

look and that angry words might really be an embryonic form of murder (Matthew 5:21–28).

Isaiah's contemporaries tried to relieve their consciences by coming to God with "meaningless" (literally: "empty") offerings. This hypocrisy only augmented their guilt and led to one of the most shocking statements of the Old Testament:

> *When you come to appear before me, who has asked this of you, this trampling of my courts? Stop bringing meaningless offerings! Your incense is detestable to me. New Moons, Sabbaths and convocations—I cannot bear your evil assemblies. Your New Moon festivals and your appointed feasts my soul hates. They have become a burden to me; I am weary of bearing them. (Isaiah 1:12–14)*

Ironically, it was God Himself who had originally commanded that these sacrifices and offerings be made. He had also instituted the calendar of religious festivals that Israel observed. Even when they were properly observed, however, these divinely ordained ceremonies had their limitations. In the New Testament the writer of Hebrews points out that these sacrifices never actually had the power to take away sin. Their work was purely external and could only render those who offered them ceremonially clean (Hebrews 9:13). The ceremonies and feasts that Israel observed were "only a shadow" of the work that Jesus Christ would later do (Hebrews 10:1). In fact, since they were incapable of perfecting those who offered them, the sacrifices were never really intended to alleviate the guilt of those who offered them. Instead, they served as "an annual reminder of sins, because it is impossible for

the blood of bulls and goats to take away sins"
(Hebrews 10:3–4). Their yearly reminder of sin was
intended to make God's people aware of their need
for the forgiveness that could only come through
the one acceptable sacrifice of Jesus Christ
(Hebrews 10:10).

Although we do not offer animal sacrifices, it is
still possible for us to make the same mistake that
Israel did. We can attempt to earn a right standing
in God's sight through our attendance at church or
by our involvement in its ministries. We may try to
balance out our disobedience to God in one area of
life with extraordinary devotion in another, perhaps increasing the amount that we put in the
offering plate or performing a religious ritual. We
may even attempt to manipulate God into doing
what we want by our devotional practices. Jesus
gave us an example of what this might look like
when He warned against the danger of measuring
the effectiveness of our prayer life by the number of
words used: "And when you pray, do not keep on
babbling like pagans, for they think they will be
heard because of their many words. Do not be like
them, for your Father knows what you need before
you ask him" (Matthew 6:7–8).

A corollary danger is the temptation to practice
our devotion to God only to be seen by others. It is
inevitable that others will occasionally see our prayer,
worship, and service to God. When that is our primary objective, however, such acts of devotion are
not really being offered to God (Matthew 6:1–8).

God's favor cannot be bought. We have nothing that He needs. Even if we were to attempt to
match its worth, no earthly treasury or human ef-

fort would be found sufficient. The only price that God ever placed upon His love was one that we could not afford. It was a price that He paid Himself—the blood of His Son.

Heavenly Father, I owe more to You than I can repay. The service that I offer today I offer in gratitude for all that You have done. I offer it in faith, knowing that You have already accepted me in Christ. Amen.

19

THE VINEYARD OF THE
LORD ALMIGHTY

The vineyard of the Lord Almighty is the
house of Israel, and the men of Judah are the
garden of his delight. And he looked for
justice, but saw bloodshed; for righteousness,
but heard cries of distress. *(Isaiah 5:7)*

One spring my wife and I decided to follow the
example of our neighbors and put in a garden.
This seemed like a relatively simple task—until we
got started. Although we lived in a farming community at the time, our little plot of land was
particularly sandy, making it difficult for anything
but weeds to grow well. The real problem, however, was that we had underestimated the amount of
effort that goes into a good garden. Weeds that were
pulled one day often reappeared somewhere else
the next. When one pest was eliminated, a different
breed took its place. Even harvesting our meager
crop was difficult for us city slickers. Somehow I
had the idea that everything in the garden would be
picked at the same time. Instead, I discovered that
the fruits and vegetables we had planted ripened at
different times. I had also underestimated the vol-
ume of produce that we would be able to harvest
from our small garden. How many zucchinis can
one family really eat?

The Lord also planted a garden. In Isaiah 5:7
the prophet refers to the House of Israel as a "vineyard" and to the men of Judah as "the garden of his

delight." This vineyard had been carefully prepared. It had been planted on a hillside that was naturally fertile (Isaiah 5:1). It was a site that, by all outward appearances, promised to be productive. In addition to the natural advantages of its location, the Lord took care to increase the vineyard's potential for fruitfulness by removing everything that might hinder its growth. He cleared the ground of stones. These would have obstructed the preparation of the soil for planting. Farmers often used these same stones to build a wall of protection around the vineyard. They also gathered them into heaps and trailed the vines over them, similar to the way we might use a trellis today.

In Isaiah's description of the Lord as a farmer, He also built a watchtower and a winepress (Isaiah 5:2). Watchtowers were a common feature in vineyards and were used to protect the plants. A servant, or perhaps even the farmer himself, slept in the watchtower and frightened away anyone who attempted to steal the grapes while they were ripening. The watchtower doubled as a temporary shelter during the harvesting season.

The winepress was a square or circular pit dug out of rock. After the grapes were harvested they were placed in the winepress and trampled with bare feet. A channel from the winepress enabled the grape juice to flow into the connecting winevat, where it was left to ferment. In Israel's case, however, the harvest was a disappointment. God asked, "What more could have been done for my vineyard than I have done for it? When I looked for good grapes, why did it yield only bad?" (Isaiah 5:4). Despite all God's efforts, the vineyard only produced rotten grapes, or as the Hebrew text literally says, "stinking" or "worthless" grapes.

Isaiah's description was not meant to be taken literally. The vineyard represented Israel and Judah. The fertile hill stood for the Land of Promise, and perhaps, more specifically, for Jerusalem itself. God had prepared the way for Israel to take root in the land by driving out the nations before them, the way a farmer might clear the stones from a field that was about to be sown with crops. He Himself had been a wall of protection around them and had repeatedly defended them against their enemies. However, instead of producing the good fruit of justice and righteousness, the vine of Israel produced only bloodshed and the desperate cry of oppression (Isaiah 5:7). Consequently, the Lord determined to destroy it:

> *Now I will tell you what I am going to do to my vineyard: I will take away its hedge, and it will be destroyed; I will break down its wall, and it will be trampled. I will make it a wasteland, neither pruned nor cultivated, and briers and thorns will grow there. I will command the clouds not to rain on it. (Isaiah 5:5–6)*

This promised destruction eventually came to pass in two phases. First, the Northern Kingdom of Israel was defeated and carried into captivity by the Assyrians in 721 B.C. after a three year siege of the capital city of Samaria. Then the Southern Kingdom of Judah fell to the Babylonians in 586 B.C. when Nebuchadnezzar stormed Jerusalem and destroyed the temple. The writer of Psalm 80 uses the metaphor of a ruined vineyard to picture this destruction. According to the psalmist, the state of God's people was like a vineyard whose walls had been broken down. Anyone who passed by could pick its fruit unhindered. Wild boars from the forest rooted through its remains, and other creatures of the field fed on what little life remained there. What was once a thing of beauty had become a burned and crumbling ruin (Psalm 80:8–16).

Jesus used the vineyard metaphor both of Israel and the church. One of His parables of the kingdom told a similar story of a landowner who had planted a vineyard, put a wall around it, built a watchtower and winepress, and then rented it out to tenants. When the time came to collect the rent, however, the tenants seized the servants that the farmer sent and had them killed. Finally, the owner sent his son, thinking that they would respect his authority, but they killed him, too (Matthew 21:33–39). When Jesus asked his listeners what the owner would do in such a case, they answered without hesitation: " 'He will bring those wretches to a wretched end,' they replied, 'and he will rent the vineyard to other tenants, who will give him his share of the crop at harvest time.' " (Matthew 21:41). Jesus agreed and predicted that God would do just that with the vineyard of Israel: "Therefore I tell you that the kingdom of God will be taken away from you and given to a people who will produce its fruit" (Matthew 21:43).

The church is God's new vineyard. It has received similar care, but with better results. Jesus has promised that the church's fruit is certain: "You did not choose me, but I chose you and appointed you to go and bear fruit—fruit that will last. Then the Father will give you whatever you ask in my name" (John 15:16). It is Christ who makes the difference between these two vines. Jesus Christ produces in the church what Israel, despite all its advantages, could not produce on its own. Jesus is the vine and all those who are connected to Him as branches must inevitably produce fruit (John 15:1–8). To ensure this, Jesus has given us the Holy Spirit, who produces His fruit within us. The Lord looked to Israel to produce the fruit of justice and righteousness. He looks to us for the fruit of love, joy, peace, patience, kindness, goodness, faithfulness, gentleness, and self-control (Galatians 5:22–23).

Lord Jesus, You are the vine and I am the branch. Use the circumstances I face today to produce the fruit of the Holy Spirit in my life. Thank You that His presence guarantees that I will not be unfruitful in the way that Israel once was. Amen.

20

A PEOPLE OF UNCLEAN LIPS

"Woe to me!" I cried. "I am ruined! For I
am a man of unclean lips, and I live among a
people of unclean lips, and my eyes have seen
the King, the Lord Almighty." *(Isaiah 6:5)*

Samuel did not want to preach. He wanted to be
a farmer. As a student in college, Samuel's least
favorite class had been public speaking. His professor charged a fine each time one of his students
skipped class the day he or she was scheduled to
make a presentation, and Samuel happily paid the
fine each time it was his turn. One chapel service,
however, he received the call he had been dreading.

"I don't even remember who the speaker was
or what he was talking about at the time," Samuel
later told me. "I just remember sensing the Lord
saying to me, 'I want you to preach.' I was sitting
way up in the balcony, and after everyone left I
stayed and wrestled with the Lord."

"Lord," Samuel had argued, "I don't want to
preach. I want to be a farmer."

"No," came the reply, "I am calling you to be a
pastor."

"But I don't want to be a pastor," Samuel objected. "I want to farm."

"I am calling you to be a pastor."

This went on for several hours. The more
Samuel objected, the more certain he was that God

was calling him to preach the gospel. Finally, Samuel gave in.

"OK, Lord," he surrendered, "I'll preach. But you are losing a very good farmer and getting a very poor preacher in the bargain!"

As it turned out, Samuel wasn't as bad a preacher as he expected. He served the Lord faithfully for many years in several small churches and then later as a missionary to Japan. He even returned to Japan after his retirement and served God there for several more years.

The prophet Isaiah felt a similar reluctance when God called him to be a prophet. Isaiah was originally from Jerusalem and may even have been part of the royal family. According to Jewish tradition he was the cousin of King Uzziah. He was also married to a woman who exercised the gift of prophecy (Isaiah 8:3). Isaiah's call to the ministry came in the year of King Uzziah's death (Isaiah 6:1). Uzziah (also called Azariah in the Scriptures) had a long and largely prosperous reign (2 Kings 14:21; 15:1–4). His successes, however, led to a dangerous attitude of spiritual pride: "But after Uzziah became powerful, his pride led to his downfall. He was unfaithful to the Lord his God, and entered the temple of the Lord to burn incense on the altar of incense" (2 Chronicles 26:16). The offering of incense was a responsibility that God had restricted to the priests. The Lord had made very clear that kings were not permitted to assume the responsibilities of the priesthood when he rejected Saul, Israel's first king, after he offered sacrifices at Gilgal (1 Samuel 13:7b–14).

When Azariah the high priest and eighty other

courageous priests confronted Uzziah, he raged at
them and was immediately struck with leprosy.
This disease made him ceremonially unclean. As a
result, he lived the remainder of his life under vir-
tual house arrest, confined to the palace and exiled
from the temple. As harsh as this may seem to us,
Uzziah was fortunate that he had been stopped in
the act. Otherwise he probably would have died
immediately. Uzziah's isolation continued even after
his death when those who buried him refused to
entomb his body with the other kings because of
his leprosy (2 Chronicles 26:23).

During these spiritually uncertain times Isaiah
saw a vision of God in human form. In contrast to
Uzziah's disgrace, Isaiah saw the Lord "seated on a
throne, high and exalted" (Isaiah 6:1). The skirt of
His robe filled the temple, and He was attended by
terrifying angelic beings that called out to each other and declared God's holiness in voices that made
the pillars of the temple shake. The sight of God's
glory made Isaiah acutely aware of his sin. Overwhelmed, he cried: "Woe to me! I am ruined! For I
am a man of unclean lips, and I live among a people of unclean lips, and my eyes have seen the
King, the Lord Almighty" (Isaiah 6:5). One of the
seraphs responded by taking a live coal from the altar and touching Isaiah's mouth with it. The fact
that the angel used tongs to pick up the coal may
indicate that it was too hot even for him to touch
without being burned.

Why did the seraph use a coal from the altar,
when cleansing was usually associated with the sacrifice that was placed upon the altar? On the day of
atonement the High Priest was to take a censer full

of burning coals from the altar and two handfuls of fragrant incense and offer it to the Lord in the Most Holy Place (Leviticus 16:11–14). In Isaiah's case, however, it was not incense that was added to the coals but the prophet himself. Whatever the angel's purpose behind the action, Isaiah clearly understood that he was being called to offer himself to God: "Then I heard the voice of the Lord saying, 'Whom shall I send? And who will go for us?' And I said, 'Here am I. Send me!'" (Isaiah 6:8).

Isaiah's assessment of himself was correct. He was useful to God only after his own sin had been dealt with. However, once cleansed, Isaiah offered his services to God without hesitation. His experience serves as a model for us. Only those who have a clear sense of their own sinfulness and the power of God's forgiveness are truly qualified to tell others of their need for salvation through Christ. They can do this because they have experienced God's remedy firsthand. Like Isaiah, believers have been called to offer their bodies as a living sacrifice (Romans 12:1–2). One element of this sacrifice is the offering of our tongues in service to God: "Through Jesus, therefore, let us continually offer to God a sacrifice of praise—the fruit of lips that confess his name" (Hebrews 13:15).

Holy Lord, use my words today as an instrument of praise and proclamation. The whole earth is full of Your glory. Glorify Yourself through me. Amen.

21

IMMANUEL'S LAND

> Because this people has rejected the gently
> flowing waters of Shiloah and rejoices over
> Rezin and the son of Remaliah, therefore the
> Lord is about to bring against them the
> mighty floodwaters of the River—the king of
> Assyria with all his pomp. It will overflow all
> its channels, run over all its banks and sweep
> on into Judah, swirling over it, passing
> through it and reaching up to the neck. Its
> outspread wings will cover the breadth of
> your land, O Immanuel! *(Isaiah 8:6–8)*

Immanuel, one of the names of Israel's Messiah,
literally means "God with us." It was revealed to
King Ahaz of Judah by the prophet Isaiah when
Jerusalem was being threatened by the united
armies of King Rezin of Aram and King Pekah of Israel. Rezin and Pekah had joined forces to resist the
growing influence of Assyria in Palestine, and they
viewed Ahaz as a potential Assyrian ally. Pekah had
hoped to replace Ahaz with a puppet ruler who
would do his bidding (Isaiah 7:6). Although Pekah
and Rezin had been unsuccessful in their initial attempt to take Jerusalem, Ahaz was so terrified by
their combined threat that "the hearts of Ahaz and
his people were shaken, as the trees of the forest are
shaken by the wind" (Isaiah 7:2).

The Lord sent Isaiah to Ahaz to allay the king's
fear and to reassure him that the Northern Kingdom of Israel would soon be "too shattered to be a

people" (Isaiah 7:8). The prophet's reassurance concluded with a warning and an unusual offer. He reminded Ahaz of the need to stand firm in his faith, warning: "If you do not stand firm in your faith, you will not stand at all" (v. 9). This condition was so important that the Lord also offered to bolster the king's faith with a sign chosen by Ahaz himself. However, instead of making the request, Ahaz declined, implying that to do so would "put the Lord to the test" (Isaiah 7:12).

The king's pious-sounding answer was both disobedient and hypocritical. Ahaz had been commanded by God to choose a sign. He preferred, instead, to place his hope in the military might of Assyria. Moreover, his apparent regard for Isaiah's God was purely superficial. Past actions had already demonstrated that he was really a pagan at heart. Ahaz regularly offered sacrifices to foreign gods in the high places and had gone so far as to offer his own son as a sacrifice to the god Molech. Later in his reign, Ahaz would replace the bronze altar used for burnt offerings with one based upon pagan design (2 Kings 16:1–18).

Despite Ahaz's refusal, the Lord promised a sign that would have implications both for the immediate future and for a generation that would not be born until centuries after Ahaz's death: "Therefore the Lord himself will give you a sign: The virgin will be with child and will give birth to a son, and will call him Immanuel" (Isaiah 7:14). This prophecy referred in the immediate context to a child that would be born to Isaiah when he married his second wife (Isaiah 8:3–4). It promised that the threat of Israel's Northern Kingdom would disappear "before the boy knows enough to reject the wrong and choose the right" (Isaiah 7:16). However, Matthew 1:22–23 indicates that this prophecy ultimately pointed to the birth of Jesus Christ as Israel's Messiah.

Few other names so aptly describe the unique nature of Jesus Christ. Since He was born of a woman, Jesus was human. However, the unique nature of His birth—conceived by the Holy Spirit by a virgin—also ensured that He would be divine. Jesus was Immanuel in the truest sense! He was God in the flesh (John 1:1, 12). As the Messiah, the right to rule over Israel and Judah ultimately belonged to Him. He was the promised heir to the throne of David who would one day rule over a reunited Judah and Israel (Isaiah 9:7; Ezekiel 37:15–25). Yet Jesus was also the Creator and the one to whom the land over which these kings were fighting truly belonged (John 1:3; cf. Leviticus 25:23).

The child to be born to Isaiah and the prophetess was also to be called Maher-Shalal-Hash-Baz (Isaiah 8:3). This curious sounding name literally meant "quick to the plunder, swift to the spoil." Prior to the birth of the child, Isaiah had written this name at the top of a large scroll (Isaiah 8:1). The presence of witnesses at this event suggests that this document was some kind of legal transaction, perhaps a property deed or even a marriage contract. The name Maher-Shalal-Hash-Baz foreshadowed the imminent threat posed by the Assyrians. Israel had rejected the Lord, depicted by Isaiah as a gently flowing stream, in favor of Rezin of Damascus. Ahaz had also rejected the Lord in favor of help from

Assyria. Both would suffer from the overwhelming flood of Assyrian aggression. As a result Samaria would eventually be destroyed and Judah would find itself in trouble "up to the neck" (Isaiah 8:7–8).

Even though Judah and Israel were on opposite sides militarily, they both made the same mistake. Each offered the trust that rightly belonged to God to something less than God. It is not wrong to use the ordinary resources that God has given to us. He expects us to use our reasoning, to take the initiative, and to plan for the future. It would not even have been wrong for these kings to use an appropriate military strategy to defend themselves against their enemies. However, whenever we allow these ordinary resources to become the source of our confidence, we practice a form of idolatry:

> This is what the Lord says: "Let not the wise man boast of his wisdom or the strong man boast of his strength or the rich man boast of his riches, but let him who boasts boast about this: that he understands and knows me, that I am the Lord, who exercises kindness, justice and righteousness on earth, for in these I delight," declares the Lord. (Jeremiah 9:23–24)

In the end, Judah had to be protected from the very military power upon which it depended for deliverance. Isaiah warned the nations that had come against Judah that they would eventually be shattered, but not because of Judah's military prowess or its strategic alliances: "Devise your strategy, but it will be thwarted; propose your plan, but it will not stand, for God is with us" (Isaiah 8:10). Judah would be protected, not so much for Judah's sake, but because it was Immanuel's land.

We too are Immanuel's personal property. All that we have comes from Him and is to be used for His glory. Because our God is with us and dwells within us, we can do all that He calls us to do (Philippians 4:13).

Immanuel, thank You for Your presence in my life. Help me to trust only in You. I know that everything I have—my intellect, my skills, and my material resources—all comes from You. Guide me today as I use them for Your glory. Amen.

22

THE PEOPLE I FORMED FOR MYSELF

Forget the former things; do not dwell on the past. See, I am doing a new thing! Now it springs up; do you not perceive it? I am making a way in the desert and streams in the wasteland. The wild animals honor me, the jackals and the owls, because I provide water in the desert and streams in the wasteland, to give drink to my people, my chosen, the people I formed for myself that they may proclaim my praise. *(Isaiah 43:18–21)*

I was never meant to be a chemist. Despite the help of a tutor, my chemistry grades in college declined with each semester. My chief difficulty was a poor memory. No matter how many hours I spent poring over my textbooks and notes, I never seemed to be able to remember what I studied. Unfortunately, my memory didn't improve when I went on to seminary. My wife, Jane, helped me learn Greek and Hebrew vocabulary by drilling me, but when test time came, she usually knew the material better than I did!

God's people also suffered occasional memory lapses. In times of prosperity they forgot that God was the source of their blessings (Deuteronomy 8:11–18). In times of trouble they forgot how God had delivered them in the past. In Isaiah 43:18, however, the Lord actually urged His people to forget the things He had done in the past. This was not an absolute prohibition. In fact, the command was itself prefaced by a reminder of the past (Isaiah 43:16). The God who had made a way through the sea and had destroyed Pharaoh's army was about to do something entirely new. For this reason, God's people were not to "dwell" on the past (Isaiah 43:18).

Normally it is a good thing to remember the way God has worked in the past. It becomes a hindrance only when it blinds us to what God is doing in the present. This is often true of churches. Some churches point back to a glorious past when the pews were filled with worshipers or to a beloved pastor whose sermons had the power of Spurgeon or Moody. This focus on the past can become unhealthy and lead to an unwise devotion to ministry methods that are no longer effective. When this happens churches continue to promote old programs because they were part of their "golden era."

This does not mean that focusing on the past is automatically bad. Israel's former experiences could teach much about the nature and character of God. They showed that He was able to guide and protect His people, even in the worst of circumstances. They provided a kind of blueprint upon which Israel could base its expectations for the future. The Lord promised to make a road for Israel through the "desert" by rescuing them from Babylonian captivity, just as He had made a road through the sea when He rescued them from slavery in Egypt (Isaiah 43:16). He also promised to provide "water in the desert and streams in the wasteland" (v. 19) just as He had done during their trek through the wilderness (Exodus 17:6; Numbers 20:8–11; Deuteronomy 8:15). The new thing that God was about to do would sprout up like the new growth of a plant or a tree.

The captivity of Judah by the Babylonians would not mean the end of Israel's hopes. This seemingly "dead" nation would sprout to life again when God restored His people to the Land of Promise (Isaiah 43:6).

Israel's chief problem was that it had forgotten how to be grateful. Instead of appreciating all that God had done, they had grown weary of worship. They saw worship as a "burden" imposed upon them by God, and they had begun to grow lax in their expression of it (Isaiah 43:23). As a result, they neglected the burnt offerings prescribed by the Law of Moses. These were offerings that were entirely consumed by the fire of the altar (Leviticus 1:9). The people failed to bring offerings of grain and incense (Leviticus 2:1–16). Sacrifices, which were meant to symbolize the need for forgiveness and the believer's complete consecration to God, were offered sullenly when they were presented to God at all.

The Israelites treated God as if He were a greedy monarch who had demanded an exorbitant sum as tribute from His poverty-stricken subjects. Because God's people had lost sight of their own sinfulness, they no longer appreciated His goodness. In response the Lord reminded Israel that, their standing before Him was a matter of grace: "I, even I, am he who blots out your transgressions, for my own sake, and remembers your sins no more" (Isaiah 43:25). They had been chosen by God, created for worship, and prepared for this calling by the experience of God's grace.

It is important to remember that worship is not the rent we pay to maintain our relationship with God. When we view things like daily Bible reading, prayer, and church attendance as the price that must be paid to stay close to God, our devotional lives soon dry up. These things are important and should be practiced with discipline, but when they are observed in a purely mechanical way they can obscure our vision of God. Intimacy with Him then becomes nothing more than a matter of doing the right thing at the right time. Instead, our worship must be fueled by a knowledge of who God is and a dual awareness of how God has worked in the past and of what He has promised to do for us in the future. The memory of how God has worked in the past makes us grateful, because it reminds us of how much we have been forgiven (Luke 7:36–48).

Knowledge of God's promises fills us with hope and enables us to worship with expectation. This hope, in turn, enables us to persevere in the midst of difficulties because we know that God is using our circumstances to transform our character (Romans 5:1–5). Although God is the ultimate focus of worship, the worship experience is never one-sided. The Westminster Larger Catechism states that "Man's chief and highest end is to glorify God and fully to enjoy Him forever." If worship has become drudgery, it may mean that we have become so caught up in the mechanics of worship that we have lost sight of the One who is its focus. The real secret to enjoying worship is to enjoy God.

God of Grace, never let me forget what You have done for me. Help me to fix my hope on the grace that is to be revealed in me when Jesus Christ returns. Help me to fulfill the calling for which I have been created: to declare Your praise in word and deed. Amen.

23
JESHURUN

> This is what the Lord says—he who made you, who formed you in the womb, and who will help you: Do not be afraid, O Jacob, my servant, Jeshurun, whom I have chosen. *(Isaiah 44:2)*

If God were to give you a new name, what would it be? I once asked this question to a group of college students and was shocked by the answers they gave. The names they suggested were overwhelmingly negative—names like "Loser" and "Unfaithful." I was struck by the difference between their answers and the biblical examples of those whose names really were changed by God. On those occasions when God chose a new name for His servants, the new name usually had a positive meaning. For example, the Lord changed Abram's name to Abraham (Genesis 17:5). Abram meant "Exalted Father." Abraham meant "Father of Many." His wife Sarai's name was changed to Sarah, which meant "Princess." Abraham's grandson, Jacob, was renamed Israel by the Lord. Jacob meant "Deceiver," whereas Israel meant either "Let God Contend" or "He Contends With God." The name Israel was a symbol of victory: "Then the man said, 'Your name will no longer be Jacob, but Israel, because you have struggled with God and with men and have overcome'" (Genesis 32:28). Solomon was given the name Jedidiah, "Beloved of Yahweh," because the Lord loved him (2 Samuel 12:25). In the New

Testament, the name of Jesus' chief disciple was changed from Simon to Peter. Peter meant "the Rock" (Matthew 16:18).

As diverse as these names were, they all had one thing in common. They symbolized God's promises. They did not reflect characteristics that already existed in those who were so named; they pointed to something that God would do in the future. This is also true of the name Jeshurun, one of the "pet" names used by God to refer to the nation of Israel. It was based upon a Hebrew root that meant "to be straight," "upright," or "pleasing." When used of Israel, it could be roughly translated "Upright One."

This name was first used in an ironic sense in Deuteronomy 32:15. There Moses predicted Israel's future unfaithfulness to God in Canaan. He compared Israel to an overfed ox who stubbornly resists the yoke: "Jeshurun grew fat and kicked; filled with food, he became heavy and sleek. He abandoned the God who made him and rejected the Rock his Savior." There is an echo of this verse in Isaiah 44:1–3. There the Lord was again described as "he who made you, who formed you in the womb, and who will help you" (Isaiah 44:2). Although God was not referred to as "the Rock," the Lord alluded to this with the promise: "For I will pour water on the thirsty land, and streams on the dry ground; I will pour out my Spirit on your offspring, and my blessing on your descendants" (Isaiah 44:3). During Israel's journey through the wilderness, God provided water from a rock (Exodus 17:6; Numbers 20:8–11). In Isaiah 44:3, however, He did not promise to refresh Israel with water but by pouring out His Spirit upon them.

Isaiah predicted that as a result of the work of God's Spirit, Israel's behavior would finally be worthy of the name "Upright One." Instead of rebelling against God, "One will say, 'I belong to the Lord'; another will call himself by the name of Jacob; still another will write on his hand, 'The Lord's,' and will take the name Israel" (Isaiah 44:5). Pagan worshipers sometimes carved or branded marks on their hands as a sign of religious devotion. A similar custom will be practiced by the followers of the Antichrist during the Tribulation (Revelation 13:16; 14:9–10; 20:4).

In the Old Testament, Moses commanded God's people to "write" the Law on their forehead and hands (Exodus 13:9; Deuteronomy 6:8; 11:18). Although this was probably only a figure of speech intended to emphasize the need to be mindful of God's law, later Judaism took it literally. Worshipers began wearing small boxes that contained Scripture texts written on parchment scrolls. These were bound on the arm and the forehead during prayer. Jesus criticized some of the religious leaders of His day for this practice, noting that their primary reason for doing so was to be seen by others (Matthew 23:5).

The prediction of Israel's return to the Lord remains to be fulfilled and will take place when the remnant of Israel is saved at the Second Coming of Christ. The church, however, has already begun to experience the blessings of the outpouring described by Isaiah. It is the ministry of the Holy Spirit that enables the Christian to be mindful of God's Word. He reminds us of what God has said in His Word (John 14:26). He reveals truth to us and enables us to understand the Scriptures (John 16:13–14; 1 John 2:27). He is the seal that marks us as God's children (Ephesians 4:30). He provides an inner assurance that we have been forgiven and belong to God (Romans 8:16). He prays for us (Romans 8:26). The Holy Spirit transforms us, enabling us to live in a way that is pleasing to God (Galatians 5:16, 22–26). In this way the Holy Spirit enables us to keep God's Word close to our minds and hearts.

This does not mean that we are perfect. The transformation that begins when we trust in Jesus as Savior and Lord will not be completed until we are in the presence of Christ. One of the ministries of the Holy Spirit is to help us wait for Christ to finish His work in us: "But by faith we eagerly await through the Spirit the righteousness for which we hope" (Galatians 5:5). This means that those of us who come to Christ for righteousness experience it in a threefold sense. When we trust in Christ we are immediately declared righteous (Romans 3:21–22; 4:5; 4:16–5:2).

As the fruit of the Holy Spirit becomes more and more evident in our lives, the evidence of righteousness is seen in our actions (1 John 2:29; 3:7). However, although this transformational power belongs entirely to God's Spirit, we also bear some responsibility in this process. We must choose to put off the old self "and to put on the new self, created to be like God in true righteousness and holiness" (Ephesians 4:24). Finally, when Jesus Christ returns, we will be given new bodies that are no longer susceptible to sin, and we will live in a new heaven and new earth, which the apostle Peter describes as "the home of righteousness" (2 Peter 3:13).

If God were to choose a new name for you today, it would not reflect your past failures. Instead, your new name would focus attention upon God's promise to finish the transforming work begun by the Holy Spirit when you trusted in Christ. It is a work that begins and ends in righteousness.

Holy Spirit, open my eyes so that I may see the opportunities You give me each day to "put off" the old self and "put on" the new self. Thank You for Your ministry of prayer and transformation. Help me to wait eagerly for the righteousness in which I hope. Amen.

24

THE WORK OF MY HANDS

> This is what the Lord says—the Holy One
> of Israel, and its Maker: Concerning things
> to come, do you question me about my
> children, or give me orders about the work
> of my hands? *(Isaiah 45:11)*

Winston Churchill was one of the most important leaders of the twentieth century. His skill as a military strategist and orator was largely responsible for saving Great Britain from the Nazi threat. He was also an accomplished artist. One of his paintings hung in the office of publisher Henry Luce. When Churchill visited Luce, the publisher offered a mild criticism of the work. "It's a good picture," he explained, "but I think it needs something in the foreground—a sheep perhaps."

Churchill said nothing. The next day, however, Luce received a message from Churchill requesting that the painting be returned. Luce sent the picture back to Churchill, who returned it a few days later with a minor addition. In the foreground, Churchill had painted one lonely sheep.

Creative people do not always appreciate criticism. This was especially true of God the Creator, when those He had made began to criticize Him. In Isaiah 45:9 the Lord warned: "Woe to him who quarrels with his Maker, to him who is but a potsherd among the potsherds on the ground. Does the clay say to the potter, 'What are you making?' Does your work say, 'He has no hands'?" The complaints focused on God's plan to use a Gentile ruler to rescue His people from captivity in Babylon. Nearly 150 years before Cyrus's birth, Isaiah predicted that a ruler named Cyrus would be God's instrument for delivering Israel from the Babylonians. He even predicted that Cyrus would give the order to lay the foundation for a new temple in Jerusalem (Isaiah 44:28). These prophecies were fulfilled with remarkable accuracy.

The son of Cambyses I, ruler of the Persian kingdom of Anshan, Cyrus II seized the throne, conquered the Median Empire, and then went on to subdue the Lydian and the Babylonian Empires. Unlike the Babylonians, who regularly destroyed the temples and relocated the inhabitants of the countries they conquered, Cyrus made it his practice to return those who had been exiled to their homelands and rebuild their temples. In 538 B.C. he issued the following edict: "This is what Cyrus king of Persia says: 'The Lord, the God of heaven, has given me all the kingdoms of the earth and he has appointed me to build a temple for him at Jerusalem in Judah. Anyone of his people among you—may the Lord his God be with him, and let him go up' " (2 Chronicles 36:23).

Isaiah's predictions of these events claimed far more than divine foresight. They made it clear that the success of Cyrus would be the result of divine control. The Lord referred to Cyrus as His "anointed," a term used elsewhere of Israel's kings and of the Messiah. This title signified that Cyrus had been specifically chosen by God to perform this important task. It also meant that God would be the one who was ultimately responsible for the military victories that Cyrus enjoyed. The Lord promised to enable Cyrus to "subdue nations" and "strip kings of their armor." He would "open doors before him so that gates will not be shut" (Isaiah 45:1). It may have been this element that caused some to complain about God's plan. Some, like the prophet Habakkuk, had grumbled in the past when God had used Gentiles to further His purposes.

God's control over events was so absolute that He was able to use blessing and calamity alike to accomplish His purposes: "I form the light and create darkness, I bring prosperity and create disaster; I, the Lord, do all these things" (Isaiah 45:7). Although the Hebrew term that is translated "disaster" can also mean "evil," it cannot have referred to evil in a moral sense. God is not capable of sin. He does not tempt others, nor can He be tempted (James 1:13–15). Evil originated with Satan and was passed on to humanity through Adam's sin. All moral evil is generated from one of two sources: either from Satan or from the hearts of fallen men and women.

God does, however, exercise sovereign control over the sinful acts of others. For example, God was not responsible for Satan's attempts to cause the patriarch Job to curse Him, but He did set limits that restricted Satan's access (Job 1:1–12; 2:1–6). Satan could go no further than God allowed. Every calamity that Job experienced passed first through the watch-care of God's loving purpose.

There are many things that cause us to question the wisdom of God's sovereign control. The friends and family members of a Christian leader whose ministry has been cut short by an early

death wonder why so many years of potential use-
fulness for God were wasted. A young man feels
that he would serve Christ better if he were married
and grows frustrated when God does not lead him
to the "right" one. A couple grows bitter through
years of unsuccessful attempts to have children
when they see the lives of so many others snuffed
out by abortion. God's plans do not always make
sense to us. Nor are His purposes always clear. We
think that an explanation from Him might help us
to bear with the pain of calamity, but would it really? Would Job have felt better during his months of
suffering if he had heard God discussing his case
with Satan before the first calamity fell?

When God responded to those in Isaiah's day
who criticized His sovereignty, He did not defend
His plan. Instead, He reminded them of His authority. He was the potter. Compared to Him, all others
were "but a potsherd among the potsherds on the
ground" (Isaiah 45:9). The potsherd had no right to
complain about the work of the potter. Nor did it
have any ability to shape its own destiny. The clay
was entirely dependent upon the skill of the potter's
hands. Fortunately, the maker of Israel was both
skilled and compassionate. Although the instruments He used to accomplish His plans did not
always act in righteousness, they could not thwart
His righteous purposes (Isaiah 45:13).

We too have the comfort of knowing that we
are the work of God's hands. The skill of the heavenly potter is so great that even the smallest events
that pass through our lives become tools to serve
His purposes. He uses the actions of believers and
unbelievers alike. We also have the comfort of

knowing His motives, because "we know that in all things God works for the good of those who love him, who have been called according to his purpose" (Romans 8:28). God does not need our advice. We are fortunate that He does not take it when it is offered. Otherwise we might mar a masterpiece.

Maker of Israel, You are my Creator. I place my life in Your hands today without reservation. Take it and shape it as You wish. Use every circumstance, whether good or bad, to bring glory to Your name. Amen.

25

MY AFFLICTED ONES

Shout for joy, O heavens; rejoice, O earth;
burst into song, O mountains! For the Lord
comforts his people and will have compassion
on his afflicted ones. (Isaiah 49:13)

The worst pain of suffering may not be physical
pain but the anguish of doubt that often ac-
companies it. Cambridge professor and Christian
apologist C. S. Lewis experienced this after he lost
his wife to cancer. In the months that followed her
death, Lewis kept a journal to help him understand
his feelings of grief. One of his first observations
was that his sense of loss seemed to overshadow the
awareness of God's presence that he had felt prior
to his wife's death.

"When you are happy, so happy that you are
tempted to feel His claims upon you as an interrup-
tion, if you remember yourself and turn to Him
with gratitude and praise, you will be—or so it
feels—welcomed with open arms," he said. "But go
to Him when your need is desperate, when all other
help is vain, and what do you find? A door
slammed in your face, and a sound of bolting and
double bolting on the inside. After that, silence."[1]

Lewis's experience is by no means unique. Israel expressed similar feelings during its long
captivity in Babylon. God's people felt both abandoned and forgotten (Isaiah 49:14). However,
Israel's sufferings differed from those of Lewis in
one important respect. Lewis could not help the

fact that his wife had contracted an illness. Israel, on the other hand, had been the cause of its own sufferings (Deuteronomy 8:19–20; Isaiah 51:13). This made Israel's complaint somewhat ironic. The people of Israel complained that God had forsaken them, when in reality they had "turned their backs" on God (Isaiah 1:4). Their reaction was much like that of those Solomon described when he observed: "A man's own folly ruins his life, yet his heart rages against the Lord" (Proverbs 19:3).

Despite their unfair accusations, the Lord promised to "comfort" His people (Isaiah 49:13). He would not stand silently by while Israel suffered, even if those sufferings had been of her own making. He also promised to "have compassion on his afflicted ones." The Lord responded to Israel's charge with a question: Could a nursing mother forget her child? The implied answer was that such cases, if they occurred at all, would be extremely rare. It was even more unlikely that God would forget Israel (Isaiah 49:15). Jesus used a similar argument when teaching His disciples about God's answers to our prayers: "Which of you, if his son asks for bread, will give him a stone? Or if he asks for a fish, will give him a snake? If you, then, though you are evil, know how to give good gifts to your children, how much more will your Father in heaven give good gifts to those who ask him!" (Matthew 7:9–11).

Jesus' words imply that, although we can be certain that God will never give us a stone when we ask for bread, the bread that He gives us may look like a stone. The trouble with God's parental compassion is that it does not always come to us in the form that we want or expect. For example, most of us would prefer not to be disciplined by God. Yet divine chastening is one of the marks of adoption. Many of the hardships we suffer are actually God's way of smoothing out the rough edges in our Christian life. This kind of suffering is as indispensable as it is unpleasant (Hebrews 12:4–11). Not all suffering can be linked to sinful choices. Certainly, some of the pain we experience comes from the consequences of our own actions. Yet God may also call us to experience suffering for which we ourselves are not the cause (1 Peter 2:20–24; 3:13–18). Either way suffering is the tool God uses to shape our character.

The lesson in this passage is a simple one. Compassion is innate to God's nature. It is one of the fundamental attributes of God. What is more, God's rebuke is as compassionate as His caress. In reality the two are inseparable. To paraphrase the writer of Hebrews, God rebukes those He caresses.

When the Lord revealed His glory to Moses, He described Himself as "the compassionate and gracious God" (Exodus 34:6). He also characterized Himself as one who "does not leave the guilty unpunished" (Exodus 34:7). These two attributes are not in conflict with each other. God's compassion complements His holiness. It was holiness that moved God to hand Israel over to the Babylonians. It was compassion that compelled Him to preserve them during their captivity. The prophet Jeremiah, who personally experienced the destruction of Jerusalem and the early stages of Israel's suffering under Babylon, later wrote: "Because of the Lord's great love we are not consumed, for his compassions never fail. They are new every morning; great is your faithfulness" (Lamentations 3:22–23).

Suffering and comfort are inescapably bound together. The degree to which we experience God's comfort will be in proportion to the measure of our distress. The greater our suffering, the more comfort will be available to us from God. This experience also brings with it an important responsibility. The "Father of compassion" and "God of all comfort" comforts us so that we may be able to comfort others (2 Corinthians 1:3–7). Suffering is always preparation for ministry.

Even when His people were convinced that He had forgotten them, Israel's God carried the memory of them with Him at all times, like a man who had engraved a picture of the city of Jerusalem on the palms of his hands (Isaiah 49:16). Tattoos were forbidden by the Mosaic Law (Leviticus 19:28). Yet, figuratively speaking at least, God had permanently "marked" Himself with the image of His people. Jerusalem's walls, which were about to be breached by the Babylonian army, were constantly before Him. The truth of this metaphor is even more poignant for those who know Christ as Savior, since Jesus continues to bear the marks of His crucifixion (John 20:25). These scars provide an eternal testimony to the depth of God's love for us. In times of trouble when God seems to be silent, let them speak for Him.

Father of Mercies, comfort me in my affliction today. When I cannot sense Your presence, speak to me through the silent testimony of Christ's wounds on my behalf. Teach me the lessons of affliction so that I may be able to comfort others. Amen.

1. C. S. Lewis, *A Grief Observed* (New York: Bantam, 1961), 4.

26

YOU WHO SEEK RIGHTEOUSNESS

> Listen to me, you who pursue righteous-
> ness and who seek the Lord: Look to the
> rock from which you were cut and to the
> quarry from which you were hewn; look to
> Abraham, your father, and to Sarah, who
> gave you birth. When I called him he was
> but one, and I blessed him and made him
> many. *(Isaiah 51:1–2)*

Even a prophet sometimes becomes discouraged.
That was true of Elijah, Isaiah's predecessor by
more than a century. Elijah's depression was probably caused by a combination of factors. He had just
come through a spiritual victory by defeating the
prophets of Baal on Mount Carmel (1 Kings
18:16–46). He was also under stress. Queen
Jezebel had sent a messenger to Elijah threatening
to take his life within twenty-four hours (1 Kings
19:1–3). But the primary cause of Elijah's depression was his own sense of isolation. He had become
convinced that, out of all God's people, he alone
was faithful (1 Kings 19:14). Fortunately, he was
mistaken. The Lord reassured Elijah that there were
still seven thousand who had not bowed down to
the pagan god Baal (1 Kings 19:18).

The prophet Isaiah also spoke of a godly remnant who, despite the sins of the nation as a whole,
continued to "pursue righteousness." The wicked
would not be the only ones to suffer in the captivity.
The righteous and the unrighteous would both

suffer the same fate. This is often the case where sin
is involved. Sin's consequences are never limited to
those who have disobeyed. There are always "inno-
cent" bystanders who are affected by its fallout. To
encourage them the prophet urged, "Look to the
rock from which you were cut and to the quarry
from which you were hewn" (Isaiah 51:1). When
the temple of Jerusalem was built, white limestone
was dug from quarries located in the surrounding
hills and shaped into blocks before being brought
to the building site (1 Kings 6:7). Isaiah compared
the faithful in Israel to stones that had been cut
from the "quarry" of Abraham and Sarah.

Similar metaphors are used in the New Testament. Those who trust in Jesus Christ for eternal
life are living stones that are being built into a spiritual temple with Jesus Christ as its chief
cornerstone (1 Peter 2:4–6). They are to look to
Abraham and Sarah as examples and emulate their
faith (Hebrews 11:11–19). They are even called
"Abraham's offspring": "Therefore, the promise
comes by faith, so that it may be by grace and may
be guaranteed to all Abraham's offspring—not only
to those who are of the law but also to those who
are of the faith of Abraham. He is the father of us
all" (Romans 4:16).

According to Isaiah, the way to "pursue righteousness" is to "seek the Lord." Jesus agreed with
this perspective. He taught His disciples to seek
righteousness by seeking the kingdom of God
(Matthew 6:33). He also taught that this was something that could only be received as a gift, noting
that the Father is pleased to give the kingdom itself
as a gift (Luke 12:32). This seeking is first and fore-

most a matter of faith. It is rooted in the certainty that God "rewards those who earnestly seek him" (Hebrews 11:6).

Those who have received this gift of righteousness go on to pursue it as a habit of life. They seek after holiness. Alexander Maclaren described this pursuit as a life of consecration to God: "Holiness is consecration, that is to say, holiness is giving myself up to Him to do what He will with. 'I am holy' is not the declaration of the fact 'I am pure,' but the declaration of the fact 'I am thine, O Lord.'"[1]

Believers also seek God through prayer. God promised His people that if they would humble themselves in prayer and "seek" His face, He would forgive their sins and heal their land. Their pursuit of God had to be genuine, and known sin needed to be repented of for this restoration to occur (2 Chronicles 7:14). As far back as the Exodus, Moses had warned that attachment to idols would eventually lead to Israel's expulsion from the Land of Promise. However, he had also reassured Israel that if they sought God with all their heart, they would find Him:

> *The Lord will scatter you among the peoples, and only a few of you will survive among the nations to which the Lord will drive you. There you will worship man-made gods of wood and stone, which cannot see or hear or eat or smell. But if from there you seek the Lord your God, you will find him if you look for him with all your heart and with all your soul. (Deuteronomy 4:27–29)*

In the New Testament Jesus warned of a more subtle kind of idolatry: "So do not worry, saying,

'What shall we eat?' or 'What shall we drink?' or 'What shall we wear?' For the pagans run after all these things, and your heavenly Father knows that you need them" (Matthew 6:31–32).

It is easy to see why anxiety might arise over what we are to eat, drink, or wear. The things that Jesus mentions are not really luxuries. Jesus affirmed as much when He reassured His disciples that "your heavenly Father knows that you need them." His words provided His disciples with a much needed reality check. He pointed out, for example, that as important as all these things were, there were other things that were even more important (Matthew 6:25). As necessary as food and clothing are, when the whole person is taken into account, they are not the *most* important things in life. Jesus' words force us to consider whether the spiritual side of our lives receives the same degree of attention as the physical side.

Jesus also reminded His disciples of their importance in God's sight (Matthew 6:26). Using birds as an example, Jesus pointed out that God provides even for those who are least important in the overall scheme of the universe. If God provides for the needs of birds, who make no provision for the future by sowing and reaping, is it not even more reasonable to expect that He will do the same for His children who do make such efforts? Our importance in God's sight becomes even more apparent when we consider our limitations. Jesus asked: "Who of you by worrying can add a single hour to his life?" (Matthew 6:27). Worrying cannot add an inch to one's height, any more than it can add a day to one's life span. In fact, worrying may actually detract from both. Worrying has a way of bowing the head and hunching the shoulders. If it becomes intense enough it can even cause illness. Yet most worries are focused on things over which we have no control. That is precisely why faith is the only remedy.

When my wife and I moved to the Philadelphia area to attend seminary, our lifestyle changed radically. Prior to the move I had been a salaried employee with one of the world's leading automobile makers. As a seminary student I worked part time for minimum wage at a bookstore in the local mall. With our income literally cut in half we were forced to make some changes. We stopped ordering out for pizza on Friday nights. We no longer attended movies. We never went to restaurants. It would be a lie if I told you that we never felt the pressure of our reduced financial status. After a few months, however, it occurred to me that I had felt just as much pressure when we were making twice as much money! Apparently the amount of income that we had at our disposal was not the root issue at all. My anxiety came from a different source. Ultimately my concerns were more a question of faith than finances.

Jesus' solution is to live a one-sided life. By calling His followers to seek first the kingdom of God and His righteousness, Jesus calls us to a life that is out of balance with the rest of the world's priorities. The mark of those who seek righteousness is that they seek Christ's interests first. Will this guarantee that all our troubles will cease? Probably not. If prophets can get discouraged, then so can we. It does mean that tomorrow's troubles will come with a fresh supply of help.

Righteous Father, help me to discern the things that are truly important and not to be overwhelmed by the cares of daily life. I look to You to provide my needs, and I want to seek Your kingdom and Your righteousness first and foremost. Amen.

1. Alexander Maclaren, *A Year's Ministry* (London: Hodder and Stoughton, 1886), 79.

27

THE RANSOMED OF THE LORD

> The ransomed of the Lord will return. They will enter Zion with singing; everlasting joy will crown their heads. Gladness and joy will overtake them, and sorrow and sighing will flee away. *(Isaiah 51:11)*

In 1932 the world reacted with horror and morbid fascination when it learned of the kidnaping of the nineteen-month-old son of Charles Lindbergh. Lindbergh's solo flight across the Atlantic five years earlier had made him an international celebrity. Tragically, Lindbergh's son was murdered, even though a ransom was paid.

Because of events like this, the word "ransom" has sinister implications for many of us. Interestingly, this term is often used in a positive sense in the Bible, where it is linked with the idea of redemption. This use drew on the legal custom of accepting payment in lieu of the death sentence, or of using money to purchase the freedom of a slave. The owner of a bull that had gored someone to death could be spared the required death penalty if the amount demanded by the family was paid (Exodus 21:28–32). A female slave who had been purchased as a wife and then subsequently rejected by her master could obtain her freedom if someone, presumably a family member, paid the ransom price (Exodus 21:8). The biblical practice of ransom combined the concepts of exchange and rescue. Those who were "redeemed" in this way were spared from some fate through the payment of a price.

Moses used this term to describe Israel's rescue from slavery in Egypt. He characterized God's people as "your own inheritance that you redeemed by your great power and brought out of Egypt with a mighty hand" (Deuteronomy 9:26). Later leaders like David and Nehemiah used similar language to speak of Israel. In a very real sense, all later pleas for Israel's deliverance were based upon this initial experience of redemption. God's people recognized that by that one act of ransoming Israel, the Lord made a permanent commitment to work for Israel's redemption. They also recognized that redemption brought with it a kind of ownership. Because the Lord had ransomed Israel, it was His personal possession. He had redeemed Israel "for Himself" (1 Chronicles 17:21; Nehemiah 1:10).

God did not limit His redemptive work to the national sphere. He also redeemed individuals. In Isaiah 29:22 He is called "the Lord, who redeemed Abraham." David, who often prayed that God would redeem Israel as a nation, also asked God to redeem him personally (Psalm 25:22; 26:11). Usually the redemption requested in these prayers involved deliverance from oppression (Psalm 69:18; 119:134). The term is used in the same context in Isaiah 51:11. In the preceding verses Isaiah called on the Lord to prepare for battle:

> *Awake, awake! Clothe yourself with strength, O arm of the Lord; awake, as in days gone by, as in generations of old. Was it not you who cut Rahab to pieces, who pierced that monster through? Was it not you who dried up the*

sea, the waters of the great deep, who made a road in the depths of the sea so that the redeemed might cross over? (Isaiah 51:9–10)

This Exodus symbolism provided a vivid reminder of the Lord's unflagging commitment to His people. Israel had already been redeemed by God and would be delivered again. Isaiah promised that the redeemed would return to Jerusalem in a procession of joy. Elsewhere Isaiah revealed that the ransom price for their deliverance from Babylonian captivity would be the Gentile nations: "For I am the Lord, your God, the Holy One of Israel, your Savior; I give Egypt for your ransom, Cush and Seba in your stead" (Isaiah 43:3). Persian dominance over these nations paved the way for the victory of Cyrus over Babylon and for Israel's eventual liberation.

These Old Testament experiences set the stage for God's ultimate work of redemption through Jesus Christ. Like Israel's ransom, the Christian's redemption can be traced to a single saving event with ongoing consequences. In this case, however, the enemy was a spiritual one rather than a national foe. The oppressor was sin, strengthened by the moral demands and threatened penalty of God's law (1 Corinthians 15:56). The ransom price was the blood of Jesus Christ (1 Peter 1:18–19; Revelation 5:9).

The believer's redemption has both negative and positive dimensions. Negatively, it is a redemption from the curse of God's Law (Galatians 3:13). The Law pronounced the penalty of death upon all those caught in the grip of sin, a fate that is experi-

enced in two distinct phases. The first phase of this
penalty is the experience of physical death, which
is also the objective proof of the universality of sin
(Romans 5:12; cf. Romans 3:23). Death, although it
initially results in the cessation of physical life, does
not lead to the cessation of existence. Those who
die must also face God's judgment (Hebrews 9:27).
As long as their sin remains, that judgment can result only in eternal separation from God. The Bible
refers to this as "the second death" (Revelation
20:14–15). Jesus promised that those who put their
trust in Him would be acquitted of their guilt and
would escape this fate: "I tell you the truth, whoever hears my word and believes him who sent me
has eternal life and will not be condemned; he has
crossed over from death to life" (John 5:24).

Positively, believers have been redeemed unto
God. Christ's redemption does more than free us
from the penalty of sin; it also frees us from sin's
power. The apostle Paul described the experience
of sin as a form of slavery. The ransom paid by
Christ has freed us from that slavery and granted us
full rights as children of God (Galatians 4:5). This
new freedom has given us a dual status. On the one
hand, those of us who know Christ are no longer
slaves (Galatians 4:8–9) but are the sons and
daughters of God. We are heirs of God and co-heirs
with Christ, and we look forward to sharing in His
glory (Romans 8:17). At the same time, we are still
servants. Since we have been set free from sin, we
can now serve God (Romans 6:16–18; 1 Corinthians 7:22–23).

Theodore Sedgwick was a judge who lived
during the era of the American Revolution and

served as Speaker of the House of Representatives from 1799 to 1801. When his wife became so ill that she was unable to care for their children, Sedgwick entrusted their care to a black servant named Mumbet. However, after Mumbet attended a town meeting where she heard the Declaration of Independence being read, she went to see Theodore Sedgwick. "Sir," she explained, "I heard that we are all born equal, and every one of us has the right to be free." Conscience-stricken by her statement, Sedgwick began legal proceedings that eventually resulted in her freedom. Although she was no longer a slave, Mumbet chose not to leave the Sedgwick household. Instead, she used her freedom to serve the Sedgwick family until her death.

The work of Jesus Christ has provided us with a similar opportunity. The freedom that we enjoy is a freedom to serve. We are to follow the example of our Lord, who "did not come to be served, but to serve, and to give his life as a ransom for many" (Matthew 20:28).

Heavenly Father, do not let me forget the price that has been paid for my freedom. Open my eyes to the unique opportunities that You have given me today to serve You and my fellow believers. Amen.

28

MY DELIGHT

No longer will they call you Deserted, or name your land Desolate. But you will be called Hephzibah, and your land Beulah; for the Lord will take delight in you, and your land will be married. *(Isaiah 62:4)*

Desertion is a tragedy in any age. The vulnerability of wives in the ancient world made it doubly tragic. Desertion was widely regarded as a mark of rejection and shame. It implied that the one who had been abandoned was seriously flawed in some way. An Israelite who married a captive and then sent her away was said to have "dishonored" her (Deuteronomy 21:14). Likewise, divorce implied that the husband had found something "indecent" in his wife (Deuteronomy 24:1). This was the metaphor used by God to describe Israel's condition while in captivity: " 'The Lord will call you back as if you were a wife deserted and distressed in spirit—a wife who married young, only to be rejected,' says your God" (Isaiah 54:6).

The rejection of God's people meant the desolation of the Land of Promise. Although the people themselves were called "deserted," the land in which they lived was called "desolate." Joel used this same term to describe the "desert waste" left behind after a devastating plague of locusts (Joel 2:3). God's promises to Israel were closely tied to the land. Moses had warned that disobedience to God's Law would bring widespread destruction:

"The whole land will be a burning waste of salt and sulfur—nothing planted, nothing sprouting, no vegetation growing on it. It will be like the destruction of Sodom and Gomorrah, Admah and Zeboiim, which the Lord overthrew in fierce anger" (Deuteronomy 29:23).

Fortunately for God's people, Israel's abandonment was only temporary. Isaiah predicted that Israel's nickname "Deserted" would be changed to "Hephzibah" and that the name "Desolate" would be changed to "Beulah." Hephzibah literally meant "my delight is in her." This was the name of King Hezekiah's wife (2 Kings 21:1). The name Beulah meant "married." This image of a woman once rejected and then later accepted by her husband despite her unfaithfulness was vividly portrayed in the life of the prophet Hosea. Hosea was a contemporary of Isaiah who prophesied to the Northern Kingdom of Israel during the reign of Jeroboam (Hosea 1:1). He is most famous for his marriage to Gomer, the daughter of Diblaim, who is described as "an adulterous wife" (Hosea 1:2). Hosea's troubled marriage and his repeated attempts to restore their relationship paralleled God's own relationship with His people.

Isaiah compared Israel's future restoration to a joyful wedding ceremony: "As a young man marries a maiden, so will your sons marry you; as a bridegroom rejoices over his bride, so will your God rejoice over you" (Isaiah 62:5). In an earlier passage Isaiah had predicted that in the time of restoration Israel would feel the same pride toward her sons that a bride might feel over her jewelry (Isaiah 49:18). In Jeremiah the same metaphor is changed so that it is God who is symbolized by the image of a bride's ornaments (Jeremiah 2:32). In a sense, Israel was married both to the Lord and to the land. Because Israel was Jehovah's bride, her idolatry was viewed by God as a form of spiritual adultery (Jeremiah 13:27; Ezekiel 23:43; Hosea 2:2).

In the New Testament, bridal imagery is used to illustrate the church's purity and its relationship to Jesus Christ. Jesus is called the bridegroom, and the church is the bride of Christ (John 3:29; Revelation 21:9). Believers have been "betrothed" to Christ (2 Corinthians 11:2). At the end of time the New Jerusalem will come down out of heaven from God, "prepared as a bride beautifully dressed for her husband" (Revelation 21:2). Apparently the bride is responsible for some of this preparation. She is pictured as being adorned in fine linen, which symbolizes "the righteous acts of the saints" (Revelation 19:8).

These two are not really in contradiction to each other. It is only Christ's work that makes the deeds of the saints righteous. The believer is saved by grace through faith in Jesus Christ apart from works (Ephesians 2:8–9). The good works that comprise the "righteous acts" by which Christ's bride prepares herself are really an outgrowth of God's workmanship: "For we are God's workmanship, created in Christ Jesus to do good works, which God prepared in advance for us to do" (Ephesians 2:10). It is Christ's own work that enables Him to "present her to himself as a radiant church, without stain or wrinkle or any other blemish, but holy and blameless" (Ephesians 5:27).

It would be a mistake to think of the metaphor

of the bride and bridegroom as being nothing more than poetic symbols that help us to understand the mystical relationship between Christ and the church. It also provides an important example to follow. When the apostle Paul worked out the practical implications of this metaphor for believers, he applied it to the marriage relationship. He compared the role of the husband to that of Jesus Christ and the role of the wife to that of the church. Both are called to submit to each other. For the wife, submission takes the form of following her husband's leadership. For the husband, submission means leading his wife in a sensitive and understanding way (Ephesians 5:21–25). The apostle Paul also noted that just as Christ and the church are united, the husband and wife are "one flesh" (Ephesians 5:29–30). This means that whenever I act selfishly toward my spouse, I am really hurting myself.

Christian marriages that follow the biblical pattern provide the world with a living analogy of what it means to belong to Christ. In an age where husbands and wives are equally prone to abandon each other, it is critically important that we accurately reflect the loving commitment of Jesus Christ to His bride. He is the One who has promised that He will never leave us or forsake us (Matthew 28:20; Hebrews 13:5).

Heavenly Bridegroom, show me how I can best prepare myself for the day when I will be joined to You. Help me to reflect Your loving commitment in my earthly relationships. Amen.

29

THE SHEEP OF MY PASTURE

"Woe to the shepherds who are destroying and scattering the sheep of my pasture!" declares the Lord. (*Jeremiah 23:1*)

At first glance a shepherd may seem like an unlikely role model for a leader. It was certainly not the image Israel had in mind when God's people chose their first king. They looked first for a hero—someone with the natural strength and fierce courage to lead them in victory against their enemies. Saul seemed like a good candidate, if only because of his height. Saul literally stood head and shoulders above the rest of his countrymen. According to 1 Samuel 9:2, Saul was "an impressive young man without equal among the Israelites—a head taller than any of the others." Saul was also a good fighter. One of his first acts as king was to rally Israel to rescue the people of Jabesh Gilead from the Ammonites (1 Samuel 11:1–11).

Despite these assets, Saul had two major flaws that eventually disqualified him for leadership. One was his tendency to act rashly. Ordered to wait for Samuel at Gilgal while preparing for battle with the Philistines, Saul became anxious when the prophet's arrival was delayed and his soldiers began to desert. In a foolish attempt to bolster their courage, Saul offered up the burnt offering, a task that the Law had restricted to Israel's priests (1 Samuel 13:7–14). Saul's other flaw was his tendency to be more concerned about the opinion of

his subjects than he was about the opinion of God.
This weakness became apparent when he was ordered by God to attack and utterly destroy the
Amalekites. Fear of popular opinion prompted him
to disobey (1 Samuel 15:1–29).

David, Israel's second king, was Saul's opposite
in many respects. Far from being the obvious choice
as Saul's successor, he wasn't even invited to attend
the feast where God's prophet planned to anoint Israel's next ruler (1 Samuel 16:1–13). There may
have been several reasons for this oversight. One factor might have been David's age. Perhaps his father
considered him too young to be concerned with
anything Samuel might have to say. A more likely
possibility was that David was overlooked out of ne-
cessity. He had an important job to do. While the
others were enjoying the feast, David was watching
over his father's flock (1 Samuel 16:10–11).

The main thing that set David apart from Saul,
however, was his responsiveness to God's Spirit.
David was a man after God's own heart who had
learned to depend upon God while watching over
his father's sheep (1 Samuel 13:14; 17:34–37).

Unfortunately, most of the rulers who followed
were more like Saul than like David. Through the
prophet Jeremiah, the Lord compared Israel's rulers
to shepherds who destroy the flock and scatter the
sheep. Ezekiel used similar language to condemn
Israel's leaders: "Son of man, prophesy against the
shepherds of Israel; prophesy and say to them:
'This is what the Sovereign Lord says: Woe to the
shepherds of Israel who only take care of themselves! Should not shepherds take care of the
flock?'" (Ezekiel 34:2).

A shepherd's primary function was to serve the flock. Shepherds provided guidance, protection, and care (Psalm 23). Israel's leaders had reversed this role. They used the flock for their own gain and ignored those who were in need (Ezekiel 34:3–5). To remedy this problem God promised to replace Israel's selfish leaders with faithful shepherds (Jeremiah 23:4). He also promised to provide His people with a new king: " 'The days are coming,' declares the Lord, 'when I will raise up to David a righteous Branch, a King who will reign wisely and do what is just and right in the land. In his days Judah will be saved and Israel will live in safety. This is the name by which he will be called: The Lord Our Righteousness' " (Jeremiah 23:5–6).

The title "Branch" was taken from one of Isaiah's descriptions of Israel's Messiah (Isaiah 11:1). It is not surprising, then, that Jesus eventually identified Himself as God's promised Shepherd. As God's ideal leader, He possessed all the characteristics that Israel's kings lacked. He was more concerned for the well-being of God's flock than for His own welfare (Matthew 9:36; Mark 6:34). He eagerly sought out those who had strayed from the flock and willingly gave His life for the sheep (Matthew 18:11–14; John 10:11).

As the Son of David, Jesus will one day rule over a restored Israel and Judah. Today, however, He watches over the church as the Great Shepherd (Hebrews 13:20; 1 Peter 2:25). Because Jesus is their model, the church's leaders are not to rule like kings, but they have been called to serve as shepherds. Like any shepherd, they must protect the flock. The apostle Paul urged the elders of the church of Ephesus: "Keep watch over yourselves and all the flock of which the Holy Spirit has made you overseers. Be shepherds of the church of God, which he bought with his own blood" (Acts 20:28).

Since they are shepherds rather than rulers, they are not to "lord it over" those God has placed in their care. This is all the more true since the flock does not belong to them. They are serving God's flock under the authority of Jesus Christ, who is the Chief Shepherd (1 Peter 5:1–4).

Where do great leaders come from? Some would say that they are born. They suggest that dynamic leaders come into the world with a personality that compels others to follow them. Others say that effective leaders are made. They are convinced that, given the right environment and training, anyone can improve his ability to lead. When it comes to the church, however, great leaders are broken. In Christ's dominion, those who rule must serve. Like the Chief Shepherd who called them, they govern by laying down their lives for the flock.

Great Shepherd, thank You for caring for my soul. Teach me to serve Your flock with the same compassion You showed during Your earthly ministry. Like David, Israel's shepherd king, make me into one who is after Your own heart. Amen.

30

THE CITY THAT BEARS MY NAME

> See, I am beginning to bring disaster on
> the city that bears my Name, and will you
> indeed go unpunished? You will not go
> unpunished, for I am calling down a sword
> upon all who live on the earth, declares the
> Lord Almighty. *(Jeremiah 25:29)*

British poet and philosopher Samuel Taylor Coleridge was once involved in a disagreement
with a friend about the task of raising children. His
opponent argued that parents should not expose
their children to religious training but should allow
them to make their own decisions about such mat-
ters when they reach the "age of discretion."
Although Coleridge strongly disagreed, he gave no
immediate reply. Instead he took his friend out into
the garden, which had been sadly neglected and
was overgrown with weeds.

"Do you call this a garden?" the man complained. "There are nothing but weeds here!"

"Well, you see," Coleridge replied, "I did not
wish to infringe upon the liberty of the garden in
any way. I was just giving the garden a chance to
express itself and to choose its own production."

Coleridge's point was clear. Training is a natural part of a parent's responsibility. Even when it is
expressed as rebuke or discipline, it is really an act
of love. The same is true of God's family. The
psalmist described divine discipline as a blessing:
"Blessed is the man you discipline, O Lord, the man

you teach from your law; you grant him relief from days of trouble, till a pit is dug for the wicked" (Psalm 94:12–13).

The biblical concept of discipline includes both negative and positive dimensions. The negative dimension of divine discipline is that of correction. When God corrects He reveals attitudes and actions within our lives that need to be changed. When He instructs He reveals the positive alternatives that must be put in their place. Divine discipline can be painful and is even compared to corporal punishment in the Scriptures. Hebrews 12:6 says that the Lord "punishes" everyone He accepts as a son, and it uses a word that literally referred to punishment by flogging. Similarly, the Lord warned in the Law of Moses that, if Israel refused to listen to His effort to rebuke them through military defeat and natural disaster, He would "afflict" them for their sins (Leviticus 26:24). This Hebrew word literally meant "to hit" or "to strike" someone or something.

Although uncomfortable, divine discipline, even in its severest form, is ultimately a sign of God's protection: "When we are judged by the Lord, we are being disciplined so that we will not be condemned with the world" (1 Corinthians 11:32). Its goal is to prompt us to engage in self-examination. When I was a student in college I worked during the summer on the assembly line of a major automobile plant in the Detroit area. I spent most of the day stamping out metal parts on a large machine and tossing them into a metal bin nearby. Every hour the foreman came over to where I was working, took a few of the parts out of the bin, and

examined them to see whether they were acceptable. This is what you and I must do when we sense
that that we are being disciplined by God. His discipline is a sign that we need to take a careful look
at our thoughts, words, and actions.

Divine discipline is a mark of ownership.
Jerusalem became the object of God's wrath because it was the city where He had placed His name
(Deuteronomy 12:11; 1 Kings 9:3). In the Christian
life, discipline is also a sign that we belong to God:
"Endure hardship as discipline; God is treating you
as sons. For what son is not disciplined by his father? If you are not disciplined (and everyone
undergoes discipline), then you are illegitimate
children and not true sons" (Hebrews 12:7–8).
Some believers mistakenly interpret divine chastening as a sign of God's rejection. Far from being an
indication that we are no longer children of God, it
provides concrete proof that we really do belong to
Him.

God's discipline in the believer's life is never an
end in itself. Its ultimate objective is transformation. For unbelievers, however, it serves a different
function. It is a signal of the inevitability of judgment. When the Lord allowed the city of Jerusalem
to be destroyed He sent a clear message, not only to
His own people, but also to the Gentile nations. If
Yahweh was willing to bring disaster upon His own
people for their sin, how could the ungodly expect
to go unpunished? This was especially true when
much of their sin had to do with their treatment of
Israel.

The apostle Peter made the same point to New
Testament believers who were suffering because of

their testimony for Jesus Christ. He warned them not to be surprised by such experiences, but to rejoice because their sufferings mirrored those of Christ. He assured them that when they were insulted because of the name of Christ they were really being blessed. Such treatment was proof that their lives reflected "the Spirit of glory and of God" (1 Peter 4:12–14). To those who were the cause of their troubles, however, the church's suffering meant something quite different: "For it is time for judgment to begin with the family of God; and if it begins with us, what will the outcome be for those who do not obey the gospel of God?" (1 Peter 4:17).

The church's suffering today is really God's warning shot, fired over the bow of a world that is largely unconcerned about His approval. It provides advance notice that a day of reckoning is swiftly approaching—a day when every man, woman, and child will be asked to account for their actions. Because they have been shielded by God's grace, those who have trusted in Jesus Christ for eternal life will be acquitted on that day (Romans 8:1). The experience of divine discipline will give them further ground for confidence, "because in this world we are like him" (1 John 4:17; cf. Hebrews 12:11). Those who do not know Christ will be condemned (2 Peter 2:6–9; Jude 14–15).

As a father, I discipline my children precisely because they *are* my children. God is no different. Those who bear His name as sons and daughters in Christ must also endure His hand. Although it may occasionally cause pain when it falls upon His own, there is never any malice in the suffering it causes. His only aim is that we may share Christ's glory.

Loving Father, thank You that I am called by Your name. Make me responsive to the loving touch of Your hand. Give me understanding when You discipline me, and use such experiences to conform me to the image of Christ. Amen.

31

ZION FOR WHOM NO ONE CARES

> "But I will restore you to health and heal
> your wounds," declares the Lord, "because
> you are called an outcast, Zion for whom no
> one cares." (*Jeremiah 30:17*)

P rior to the coming of Jesus Christ as Messiah, Israel's relationship with God was largely defined
by two major events. The first was Israel's birth as a
nation in the Exodus. Throughout the Old Testament God's people looked back to their rescue from
Egyptian slavery as the preeminent proof of God's
love for them and as the prototype for all future experiences of deliverance. The second major event
that defined Israel's relationship with God was the
fall of Jerusalem. Without a doubt, this was Israel's
greatest trauma. If the Exodus was Israel's ideal of divine deliverance, the fall of Jerusalem became the
epitome of God's judgment. Jews and Gentiles alike
viewed it as a sign of Yahweh's rejection of His people. Jeremiah noted that, as a result of this, some had
referred to the nation of Israel as "an outcast" (Jeremiah 30:17). Jeremiah used this term elsewhere to
compare Israel to a flock that had been driven from
its pasture by lions: "Israel is a scattered flock that lions have chased away. The first to devour him was
the king of Assyria; the last to crush his bones was
Nebuchadnezzar king of Babylon" (Jeremiah 50:17).
The same word was used of David's son Absalom after he was banished from Jerusalem for murder
(2 Samuel 14:13).

Those who had seen Jerusalem's destruction also referred to the city as "Zion for whom no one cares" (Jeremiah 30:17). The Hebrew term for the word "care" is one that literally meant "to seek." It is the word David used when he complained: "Look to my right and see; no one is concerned for me. I have no refuge; no one cares for my life" (Psalm 142:4). In Israel's case, however, it was not merely the abandonment of friends that caused such distress, but the sense that Yahweh Himself had abandoned His people. This was partially true. God's decree had made the Israelites outcasts from the Land of Promise (Jeremiah 8:3; 16:15; 23:3, 8; 32:37). However, although it was true that He had rejected them temporarily, He had not abandoned them permanently. The Lord had predicted that He would eventually restore Israel to its inheritance and promised to manifest His presence to His people while they were in exile. God reassured the exiles that He would continue to be a sanctuary to His people even after the Babylonians destroyed the sanctuary in Jerusalem (Ezekiel 11:16).

God's real desire for His people was restoration. He promised to "restore" them to health and to "heal" their wounds (Jeremiah 30:17). Israel's rejection and subsequent suffering were really just means used by God to achieve that end. According to Jeremiah, God's promised restoration would involve five important features:

A Restoration of Fortune—God promised to "restore the fortunes of Jacob's tents and have compassion on his dwellings" (Jeremiah 30:18). The people of Israel would return to the land out of which they had been driven. The ruins of Jerusalem would be rebuilt, and the city would once again become a center for worship. This prophecy has already been partially fulfilled—first by the return to Jerusalem of a remnant during the reign of Cyrus, and then later by Jews in the twentieth century. Its ultimate fulfillment, however, will take place during the Millennium, when Jesus Christ will be finally recognized as Israel's Messiah.

A Restoration of Joy—Jeremiah predicted that the return of God's people to the land of Israel would be an occasion for praise and thanksgiving. The rebuilt city would resound with "songs of thanksgiving and the sound of rejoicing" (Jeremiah 30:19).

A Restoration of Community—Jerusalem's population would be decimated when the city finally fell and its citizens were deported. The Babylonians followed the practice of their Assyrian predecessors and regularly deported a significant portion of the population of those cities they captured in battle. The children of Jewish nobility were among the first to be taken to Babylon. This included Daniel and his friends Hananiah, Mishael, and Azariah (Daniel 1:11). Jeremiah promised, however, that in the future Jerusalem would once again be a flourishing city filled with children (Jeremiah 30:20).

A Restoration of Justice—Even though the Babylonians were the instruments God planned to use to discipline His people, they were still accountable to Him for their actions. Because of this, the Lord promised to punish Israel's oppressors. He also promised to place a ruler over His people who would "arise from among them" (Jeremiah 30:21).

A Restoration of Fellowship—Many of Israel's

sufferings were caused by the unfaithfulness of its rulers. Jeremiah predicted that the Messiah, God's chosen leader, would be different. His leadership style would be marked by a genuine intimacy with God. Jeremiah also promised that this blessing of intimacy with God was to be shared by the people at large. Once restored, they would again experience a sense of God's presence and enjoy the blessings that came with their status as the people of God. The Lord sealed this promise with the words: "So you will be my people, and I will be your God" (Jeremiah 30:22). These words were first spoken to Moses when the Lord told him of His plan to rescue Israel from the Egyptians (Exodus 6:7; cf. Leviticus 26:12).

Although these promises focus primarily on the national blessings to be given to the remnant of Israel, they also offer a clear portrait of what restoration to fellowship with God looks like in the Christian life. The work of Christ has restored to us the inheritance once lost through Adam's sin. Those who have placed their faith in Jesus as Lord and Savior look forward to "an inheritance that can never perish, spoil or fade—kept in heaven for you, who through faith are shielded by God's power until the coming of the salvation that is ready to be revealed in the last time" (1 Peter 1:4–5).

The believer's righteous standing with God is the basis for our worship. It is the reason we can speak to one another with psalms, hymns, and spiritual songs (Ephesians 5:19). Our confidence that God will hear our prayers and answer them enables us to make our requests with thanksgiving (Colossians 4:2).

Restoration to God has meant restoration to fellowship with one another. When we are joined to Christ we also become a part of the larger community of believers. We are all part of the household of God (Ephesians 2:19). We are assured of justice tempered with mercy, because Jesus Christ Himself has become our advocate (1 John 2:1). God is our defender and has promised never to leave us or forsake us (Hebrews 13:5–6).

Most important of all, Jesus Christ has opened the way for us to experience true intimacy with God. He has sent the Holy Spirit to assure us that we are God's children (Romans 8:15; Galatians 4:6). Although our experience of this intimacy is imperfect in this life, a day is coming when our fellowship with God will be perfect and unhindered. It is the fulfillment of this promise that the apostle John pictures at the close of the book of Revelation when the New Jerusalem descends from heaven: "And I heard a loud voice from the throne saying, 'Now the dwelling of God is with men, and he will live with them. They will be his people, and God himself with be with them and be their God' " (Revelation 21:3).

Loving Father, open my eyes today to the many evidences of Your care for me. Give me the assurance through the ministry of the Holy Spirit that I belong to You. Hasten the day when Your dwelling place will be with Your people and You will live with them. Amen.

32

A REBELLIOUS HOUSE

> The people to whom I am sending you are obstinate and stubborn. Say to them, "This is what the Sovereign Lord says." And whether they listen or fail to listen—for they are a rebellious house—they will know that a prophet has been among them. *(Ezekiel 2:4–5)*

While Benjamin Franklin was serving as an American diplomat to France, he enjoyed playing chess with the Duchess of Bourbon. During one of their games Franklin successfully placed the noblewoman's king in check and then promptly took it. The duchess objected. "We do not take kings so," she complained. Franklin, who had been one of the architects of the American Revolution, replied with a wry smile, "We do in America!"

One cynic has observed that the difference between revolution and rebellion depends upon which side you are on. The American colonies viewed the war that eventually gained them their political autonomy as a necessary struggle for independence. Great Britain, on the other hand, saw it as an act of rebellion.

There may be times when an oppressive ruler must be resisted. When it comes to God, however, any resistance is sin. According to Ezekiel 2:4, this was a recurring problem with the nation of Israel. In His commission to the prophet, the Lord described the people of Israel as "a rebellious house." God's people exhibited this rebelliousness by being "obstinate" and "stubborn." The Hebrew equivalent for the word "obstinate" is a phrase that literally means "severe of face." "Stubborn" is based upon a similar Hebrew phrase that literally means "hard of heart." This was the same characteristic that had prompted Pharaoh to resist God (Exodus 7:22; 8:15, 19, 32; 9:7, 34–35). These descriptions reveal that rebellion has both an internal and an external dimension. The internal dimension of rebellion is the attitude of the heart. The external dimension of rebellion is expressed in one's disposition.

These two aspects are related but express themselves in very different ways. The difference between being obstinate and being stubborn can be illustrated by comparing the actions of two rebellious boys. One boy was told to sit down at the dinner table. After repeated threats by his parents, he finally complied. But as he did, he quietly muttered: "I am sitting down on the outside but I'm standing up on the inside!" The other boy was told by his parents not to cross the street. Despite their threats of punishment if he disobeyed, the boy decided to cross anyway. But before he did, the boy went to his mother and said, "Mom, you might as well spank me now, because I am going to cross that street." The first boy was obstinate. He obeyed but with a disobedient heart. The second boy was stubborn. He was determined to disobey regardless of the consequences.

Rebellion against God lies at the root of every other form of sin. Yet those who are rebellious often do not perceive themselves to be so. This was true of the people of Israel. They boasted about their religious heritage and claimed to rely upon God. Yet the Lord complained that they took oaths and invoked the name of Yahweh "but not in truth or righteousness" (Isaiah 48:1). The Lord did not accept this show of religious devotion at face value: "For I knew how stubborn you were; the sinews of your neck were iron, your forehead was bronze" (Isaiah 48:4).

One of the subtlest forms of rebellion is the tendency to substitute religious devotion for genuine obedience. This was what King Saul attempted to do when he kept alive for future sacrifice animals that God had said should be destroyed (1 Samuel 15:17–21). God's prophet responded by pointing out that no animal sacrifice can compensate for disobedience: "But Samuel replied: 'Does the Lord delight in burn offerings and sacrifices as much as in obeying the voice of the Lord? To obey is better than sacrifice, and to heed is better than the fat of rams. For rebellion is like the sin of divination, and arrogance like the evil of idolatry. Because you have rejected the word of the Lord, he has rejected you as king" (1 Samuel 15:22–23).

True obedience is not merely performing the right action. It is possible to do the right thing in the wrong way. Jesus explained that the heart is the spring from which the nature of every action ultimately flows (Matthew 15:16–20). Obedience in the Christian life, then, involves more than merely complying with rules and regulations. The only kind of obedience that pleases God is obedience from the heart (Romans 6:17; Ephesians 6:6).

Israel's rebellious attitude made ministry difficult for Ezekiel. Among the first contingent to be taken to Babylon by Nebuchadnezzar, Ezekiel was

given the unpleasant task of denouncing Israel's sin
and was warned in advance that he would be resisted. Ministry to the Jewish exiles would be like
being surrounded by briers and thorns or like
sleeping on a bed of scorpions (Ezekiel 2:6). The
Lord warned Ezekiel not to let fear of their hostility
keep him from delivering his message: "You must
speak my words to them, whether they listen or fail
to listen, for they are rebellious" (Ezekiel 2:7).

The apostle Paul faced a similar challenge from
those who disliked his message. Some attempted to
persuade him to alter his gospel so that it would be
more palatable to his listeners. He was persecuted
for preaching a message that focused on Christ's
suffering as the only means of salvation (Galatians
5:11; 6:12). When the apostle became unwelcome
in Galatia because of the unpopular nature of his
message, he complained: "Even though my illness
was a trial to you, you did not treat me with con-
tempt or scorn. Instead, you welcomed me as if I
were an angel of God, as if I were Christ Jesus himself. What has happened to all your joy? I can
testify that, if you could have done so, you would
have torn out your eyes and given them to me.
Have I now become your enemy by telling you the
truth?" (Galatians 4:14–16).

In God's eyes refusing to tell the truth is as
much an act of rebellion as refusing to obey the
truth. Both replace God's authority with a human
substitute. In the case of the one who refuses to
obey God's truth, it is self that is the ultimate authority. Those who are unwilling to communicate
God's truth to others because of its unpopularity
have made the will of the crowd their ultimate

authority. We are called to speak and obey the truth.

In civil affairs, independence can be a virtue. But this is never true of our relationship to God. His demand for obedience is absolute. The obedience He desires comes from within as well as from without. By sending His Son to die for us God has provided the power to comply with all that He has commanded. The work of Christ on the cross has freed us from the tyranny of sin's power. Those who have trusted in Him are no longer slaves to disobedience but are free to obey God from the heart (Romans 6:11–14). Although those who suffer under oppressive governments may need to throw off the yoke to find freedom, in the Christian life the only way to find true independence is to put it on. Jesus urged: "Come to me, all you who are weary and burdened, and I will give you rest. Take my yoke upon you and learn from me, for I am gentle and humble in heart, and you will find rest for your souls. For my yoke is easy and my burden is light" (Matthew 11:28–30).

Sovereign Lord, create a willing heart within me so that I may offer You my unconditional obedience. I accept the easy yoke of Christ this day and look to Your Spirit for the power to obey all that You have commanded. Amen.

33

MY LOVED ONE

Say of your brothers, "My people," and of
your sisters, "My loved one." *(Hosea 2:1)*

Dan wasn't very happy to see the pastor when
he showed up. He knew without being told
what he had come to talk about. The pastor had
learned of Dan's romantic involvement with a
woman at work and had come to persuade him to
return to his wife. Dan had been planning to run
away with the new woman. In fact, he had already
purchased the plane tickets and was packing his
bags when the pastor knocked on the door. As a
courtesy, Dan let the pastor talk while he continued
to pack.

As he listened, Dan began to see his life in a
different light. He and his wife Marcy had begun to
attend church for the sake of the children. Now he
realized that he also had spiritual needs. He prayed
with the pastor and asked God to forgive him, and
he committed his life to Jesus Christ. When he was
finished, he felt like a new person. Now, however,
he was faced with a new dilemma. What if Marcy
refused to forgive him? He had done nothing to deserve her forgiveness. What would she decide?

The Old Testament prophet Hosea was asked
to make a similar choice. Hosea's story is one of the
most remarkable, and in some ways the most mys-
terious, in the Bible. It raises many questions that
cannot be easily answered. For example, was
Gomer already a prostitute when Hosea married

her? Or was he told to marry a woman who would
later be unfaithful to him? Why did God tell Hosea
to do such a thing in the first place? Was it God's
idea? Or was Hosea already in love with Gomer?
Despite these questions, one thing is clear: Hosea's
relationship with Gomer was meant to be a living
parable depicting God's relationship with Israel. Because of this, when Gomer gave birth, Hosea gave
the children symbolic names. The first child was
called Jezreel: "Then the Lord said to Hosea, 'Call
him Jezreel, because I will soon punish the house of
Jehu for the massacre at Jezreel, and I will put an
end to the kingdom of Israel' " (Hosea 1:4). Israel's
defeat was to take place in "the Valley of Jezreel"
(v. 5). King Jehu of Israel had slaughtered his predecessor King Joram while he was recovering from
wounds at Jezreel (2 Kings 9:14–26). The second
child was called Lo-Ruhamah, a name that meant
"not loved." The third was called "Lo-Ammi,"
which meant "not my people" (Hosea 1:8–9).

These names symbolized God's intention to
abandon the Northern Kingdom of Israel to the
might of Assyria. They also set the stage for a remarkable display of God's grace. Through Hosea
the Lord promised to miraculously protect Judah
and eventually reunite Judah and Israel. He
promised: "The people of Judah and the people of
Israel will be reunited, and they will appoint one
leader and will come up out of the land, for great
will be the day of Jezreel" (Hosea 1:11). This prediction looks forward to the time when Jesus Christ
would rule over a reunited Israel during the Millennium. What is more, it underscores His eternal
commitment to His people. Just as Hosea would

have been within his rights to divorce Gomer, God would have been justified in abandoning Israel forever for breaking faith with Him and violating the covenant. He had tolerated their idolatry for generations and had appealed to them repeatedly through the prophets, yet they persisted in their sin. In spite of this, the Lord continued to offer Israel His love. He promised that the day would come when He would once more refer to Israel as "my people" and "my loved one" (Hosea 2:23).

Did they deserve such treatment? Certainly not! That was precisely the point being made. Yet, regardless of Israel's unfaithfulness, it was impossible for God to deny His own nature. Although He had warned them through Moses that their unfaithfulness would eventually lead to exile, He had also promised not to forsake them: "When you are in distress and all these things have happened to you, then in later days you will return to the Lord your God and obey him. For the Lord your God is a merciful God; he will not abandon or destroy you or forget the covenant with your forefathers, which he confirmed to them by oath" (Deuteronomy 4:30–31).

Fortunately for Dan, Marcy knew what it was like to need forgiveness. She accepted him back, and they began to build a new marriage relationship with Jesus Christ at the center. Today they are both very involved in their church and have been used by God to help other struggling couples. Marcy forgave Dan, not because he deserved it, but because she had experienced God's forgiveness herself. Her decision to accept him back was an act of grace.

We are no different in our need for grace. The

New Testament even uses the language of the book of Hosea to help us appreciate God's grace in accepting us in Christ:

> But you are a chosen people, a royal priesthood, a holy nation, a people belonging to God, that you may declare the praises of him who called you out of darkness into his wonderful light. Once you were not a people, but now you are the people of God; once you had not received mercy, but now you have received mercy. (1 Peter 2:9–10; cf. Romans 9:22–26)

When God looks at us, the image He sees is one that has been refracted through the prism of His love. It is a love so powerful it can even take our past actions and transform them. As our sins pass through the work of Christ they are gloriously transformed into a rainbow of forgiveness and righteousness. We who were once "not a people" are now the beloved children of God.

Loving Father, help me to demonstrate to others the same grace that You have showed me. Place within my heart a spirit of mercy and forgiveness. Give me the patience of Christ when dealing with those who have sinned against me. Amen.

34
THE CHILDREN OF PROMISE

It is not as though God's word had failed.
For not all who are descended from Israel
are Israel. Nor because they are his descendants are they all Abraham's children. On the
contrary, "It is through Isaac that your offspring will be reckoned." In other words, it
is not the natural children who are God's
children, but it is the children of the promise
who are regarded as Abraham's offspring.
(Romans 9:6–8)

M y grandmother once claimed that her grandfather was the first to drive a twenty-mule
team across Death Valley. She was also convinced
that we had ancestors who came to America on the
Mayflower. Although I had no way of knowing
whether they were true, her stories captivated my
interest. As a result, several years later I was excited
to learn that a distant cousin was planning to write
a history of our family. She had written out a de-
tailed genealogy and planned to send my father a
copy. When it arrived I unrolled it and traced the
web-like intricacies of its many branches. I had no
idea my family tree was filled with so many inter-
esting people! I followed the lines of descent until I
finally located my parents' names. My excitement
quickly faded when I saw that the details about my
family were largely incorrect. If my cousin had been
so mistaken in her information about people who
were still alive, and whose details could be verified
with a simple phone call, how could I be confident

that she was accurate in what she said about people
long since dead?

My interest in my family's ancestry is one that
was shared by the people of Israel. The Bible con-
tains several genealogical lists. The earliest
genealogies focused on the descendants of Adam
(Genesis 4:1–26). These family histories did more
than trace lineage; they also described the accom-
plishments and spiritual history of Adam's
offspring. With the coming of Abraham, however,
genealogies took on a new significance. God had
made certain promises to Abraham and his seed
(Genesis 15:18). He had also limited those promises to Abraham's descendants through the line of
Isaac, rather than through the line of Ishmael (Genesis 21:12). Isaac was Abraham's son by his wife
Sarah (Genesis 21:1–7). Ishmael was Abraham's
son by his wife's servant Hagar (Genesis 16:1–4).

Isaac was born to Abraham in his old age,
when he and Sarah were past childbearing age: "By
faith Abraham, even though he was past age—and
Sarah herself was barren—was enabled to become a
father because he considered him faithful who had
made the promise. And so from this one man, and
he as good as dead, came descendants as numerous
as the stars in the sky and as countless as the sand
on the seashore" (Hebrews 11:11–12). Abraham's
descendants used genealogies to demonstrate the
legitimacy of their claim to a share in his inheritance by natural descent. Ironically, however, the
restriction of God's promises to the line of Isaac
over Ishmael was actually intended to show the opposite. It was an indication that God's grace

belonged to those who were "born by the power of the Spirit" (Galatians 4:29).

Genealogical lists served an additional purpose after the coming of the Law of Moses. Under the Law, priestly duties were restricted to those who were descendants of Moses' brother Aaron. When the exiles returned to Jerusalem after the Babylonian captivity, priests had to prove that they were descended from Aaron before they could serve in the reconstructed temple. Those who were unable to do so were pronounced unclean and excluded from the priesthood (Nehemiah 7:64–65). Even those who were not priests had to prove that they were "descended from Israel" (Ezra 2:59). This distinction reflected a long-standing barrier between Jews and Gentiles (Ephesians 2:14). It also led to the misconception that natural descent was all that was needed to take part in the promises made to Abraham. Many of Jesus' contemporaries believed this and boasted in the fact that they were "Abraham's children" (Luke 3:8). Jesus taught instead that in God's sight Abraham's children were those who exhibited the same faith as Abraham (John 8:39–40).

This concept of *spiritual* descent led the apostle Paul to make an important differentiation between "Abraham's offspring" and "Abraham's children" in Romans 9:6–8. He taught that physical descent did not automatically give someone the right to be considered one of "Abraham's children" (literally Abraham's "seed"): "In other words, it is not the natural children who are God's children, but it is the children of the promise who are regarded as Abraham's offspring" (Romans 9:8). This subtle distinction eliminated two of the most common benchmarks often used to claim a righteous standing before God. First of all, it eliminated family heritage. It meant that physical descent alone was not enough to guarantee that one would experience all the blessings promised to Abraham.

Certainly, there were many benefits to such a heritage. Those who could claim physical descent from Abraham had been given promises regarding the land of Israel, had received the Law, and had been given the opportunity to worship in the temple (Romans 9:4–5). Yet only those who shared Abraham's faith could claim to possess Abraham's righteousness (Romans 4:12–13).

Second, this distinction between physical and spiritual descent eliminated human effort as a means of obtaining righteousness. Paul illustrated this by pointing to God's choice of Isaac's son Jacob over his twin brother Esau "before the twins were born or had done anything good or bad" (Romans 9:11). This proved that God's acceptance was ultimately based upon grace and not upon human effort. Israel's great mistake was to pursue righteousness on other terms. Instead of seeking to obtain it by faith, they hoped to attain it by doing good works (Romans 9:30–33).

These mistakes are not limited to Abraham's descendants. Many today think being baptized into a local church or raised in a Christian home guarantees them a place in heaven. When asked about their hope of eternal life, they point to the training they received from a godly parent or to the fact that they have been attending church for as long as they can remember. Others base their confidence upon the fact that they have "led a pretty good life." A godly heritage is a great blessing and brings many advantages with it. It exposes a person to the teaching of God's Word and to people who will care enough about that person's spiritual well-being to pray for him. It is also important to do good works. Indeed, we have been designed for them (Ephesians 2:10).

Yet as important as these things are, they are not enough to gain a righteous standing in God's sight. The message of the gospel is that we are saved by grace and through faith, not by works (Ephesians 2:8–9; Titus 3:5). I should rejoice in my godly heritage and seek to please God in my actions, but it is Christ alone who can make me righteous. Only faith in Christ can guarantee whether or not I am truly one of God's children.

I am not certain whether my family line can truly be traced back to the Mayflower. I rather doubt it. I do know, however, that my lineage of faith goes back much further. My spiritual line can be traced all the way back to Abraham. Not by accident of birth or force of human effort, but because I have placed my faith in Jesus Christ. By God's grace I have become a child of God and one of those the apostle Paul labels "the children of promise."

God of Abraham, thank You for Your promise that all who trust in Jesus Christ in faith will be reckoned as righteous. By that promise I now share in the blessings of Abraham and the hope of Israel. Use me to share this same message with others. Amen.

Moody Press, a ministry of Moody Bible Institute,
is designed for education, evangelization, and edification.
If we may assist you in knowing more about Christ
and the Christian life, please write us without obligation:
Moody Press, c/o MLM, Chicago, Illinois 60610.